crafting

authentic

paper

flowers

**The beginner's guide to creating beautiful
lifelike paper blooms with step-by-step projects**

crafting

authentic

paper

flowers

The beginner's guide to creating beautiful
lifelike paper blooms with step-by-step projects

SOPHIE LONGHURST

Photographs by Zach & Grace

WHITE OWL

To my boys, Hughie, Flynn, Samson and Kit.
Everything I do is for you.

First published in Great Britain in 2021 by
PEN & SWORD WHITE OWL
An imprint of Pen & Sword Books Ltd
Yorkshire – Philadelphia

www.gingerandflynn.co.uk @gingerandflynn

ISBN 9781526784667

A CIP catalogue record for this book is available from the British Library.

Group Publisher: Jonathan Wright
Series Editor and Publishing Consultant: Katherine Raderecht
Art Director: Jane Toft
Editor: Katherine Raderecht
Photography: Zach & Grace www.zachandgrace.co.uk
Printed and bound in India, by Replika Press Pvt. Ltd.

Pen & Sword Books Ltd incorporates the Imprints of Pen & Sword Books
Pen & Sword Books Limited incorporates the imprints of Atlas, Archaeology, Aviation,
Discovery, Family History, Fiction, History, Maritime, Military, Military Classics, Politics,
Select, Transport, True Crime, Air World, Frontline Publishing, Leo Cooper, Remember
When, Seaforth Publishing, The Praetorian Press, Wharncliffe Local History, Wharncliffe
Transport, Wharncliffe True Crime and White Owl.

For a complete list of Pen & Sword titles please contact:
PEN & SWORD BOOKS LIMITED
47 Church Street, Barnsley, South Yorkshire S70 2AS, England
E-mail: enquiries@pen-and-sword.co.uk
Website: www.pen-and-sword.co.uk
or
PEN AND SWORD BOOKS
1950 Lawrence Rd, Havertown, PA 19083, USA
E-mail: Uspen-and-sword@casematepublishers.com
Website: www.penandswordbooks.com

contents

introduction

This book introduces you to the delicate art of paper flower crafting, which originated in China in 100BC when paper was first invented. The Chinese would make flowers as a meditative religious offering and send them floating down the rivers. Both paper and paper flowers were traded on the Silk Road and were used all over the world for special occasions such as weddings and fiestas. In Victorian England women took to the craft to keep themselves busy and the flowers were seen as a status symbol.

Nowadays, for me, making paper flowers is a form of creative mindfulness. I find taking time out of the day to craft and create helps me to unwind and forget the stress of the modern world. I struggle to keep still and often find myself thinking "what can I do next?" even though I am a busy mum to four boys and run my own business. Crafting paper flowers became my sanctuary and an expression of my creativity.

I am completely self-taught and want to show you ways to create authentic paper flowers, to inspire your creativity and help you take the first steps towards making your own unique floral art.

When I am making my paper flowers, I hide away amongst my treasured art supplies, which I have gathered over many years. It is a small creative space, but it's light and airy. My mood and surroundings always inspire me so, when I want to start work, I fill my diffuser with essential oil and then I am ready to concentrate on creating my paper flowers.

I live in a pretty stone cottage nestled between the seaside and moorland in Yorkshire. My natural surroundings are a huge source of inspiration for me. Working with flowers every day means I have developed a great love for their complex form and beauty.

Nature is such a wonderful thing; it can often be taken for granted but making paper flowers brings a new respect for the complexity of flowers and is a wonderful way of stopping and taking stock of the ever changing beauty of the natural world throughout the seasons.

Raising four boys in our rural cottage we spend as much time outside as possible. We are rarely put off by bad weather, and we can be found walking our four dogs or out on the horses come rain or shine.

When I can fit it around our hectic schedules I also love sea swimming; it is something that stole my heart in my childhood when I grew up playing in the sea in the nearby coastal village of Runswick Bay.

I urge anyone to get outside and into the natural world to seek inspiration from the colour changes that come with the seasons, the weather and the plants growing around you. Take a flower to study and a flower to dissect and using paper, tools and colour take apart and then try to rebuild this delicate and beautiful thing.

HOW TO USE YOUR BOOK

My number one tip when you start paper flower making is not to rush. Making flowers takes time. Once you are familiar with the different techniques, you will find some short cuts but until then don't start making your first flower expecting it will be done and dusted in no time!

Making flowers is as much about the slow enjoyment of the creative process as the finished result; it brings an element of calm in this crazy fast paced world we live in.

Secondly this book is intended to be used as a guide. It will spark your creativity and give you ideas so that you can go and create flowers yourself. You can feel a sense of achievement and pride in your own journey as you perfect your style in this art form.

Make the flowers you see around you day to day. Once you get started, you will begin to notice colours and observe petal shapes and patterns. Make notes on everything you see and what draws you to a flower. It is the subtle differences in colour, shape and aging spots that add to the realistic look you want to achieve.

I have chosen a combination of flowers I love to use in my work and some I enjoy growing in my garden. All the flowers can be used together to complement one another. They can also be displayed individually for a simple but stylish addition to your space.

At the start of the book you will find a few basic techniques which you need to master in order to create realistic looking paper flowers.

There is also a chapter detailing a list of my favourite materials. Over time you will discover which materials you favour as you develop your own techniques.

I have tried to mix up the colour palettes used in the book but, over time, you will learn to mix the colours and use the materials that work best for you. In my chapter on colours, there are lots of ideas for you to explore.

I have treated each flower project in the book like a recipe in a cookery book. I have given you some background on the flower, a list of ingredients you will need, petal patterns for you to trace and a step-by-step list of instructions and illustrations to guide you through the process.

You will find an 'essential kit bag' which details all the materials you will need to make every flower. There is also a 'you will need list' for any extras and also a colouration list - it is up to you whether you use the colour crepes I suggest or create your own colour using any medium you prefer.

materials

All you need to get started are a few basic tools like tweezers and pliers, a selection of crepe papers and vessels for paint, colour mixing, glue and water. You will also need to invest in some artist's materials like water based paints, pastels and natural dyes to colour your flowers.

YOUR ESSENTIAL KIT BAG

To make the flowers in the following chapters, you will need to gather together an essential kit bag. Most tools are easy to find online, or in specialist craft shops, and are not expensive.

- Large scissors
- Small scissors
- Stub wires (thin, medium and thick)
- Spike, skewer or thick stub wire
- Pencil
- Ruler

- Tracing paper
- Long-nose pliers
- Tweezers
- Paper creaser
- Tacky glue
- Floral tape (greens, brown and white)

CREPE PAPER

The flowers in this book are made using crepe paper. Crepe paper is heavy and gathered, which means it lends itself well to being manipulated. These gathers help to depict the veins in leaves and on petals so it is important they run in the right direction to create the most authentic look.

The only issue with crepe paper is that machine lines across the grain of the crepe can disrupt the smoothness. I try to cut in between these lines or place them at the base of my flowers, where they will be less noticeable.

You also need to be careful how you store your crepe paper and finished flowers as moisture and direct sunlight can both adversely affect the paper.

There are many different types and thicknesses of crepe paper, but don't feel intimidated. Simply start with what you can find easily and experiment to see which paper you enjoy working with and that gives you the best results.

Double sided extra fine - also referred to as doublette - is one of my favourite papers; I love its fine gathers and the delicate look it gives to petals. It is made by fusing two pieces of fine crepe together, meaning each side can be a different colour.

Extra fine - this is a delicate paper that needs only gentle manipulation which means it isn't the best paper for using with colouring or bleaching techniques.

180g Italian - I started out practicing with this crepe and I find it really good for paper flower making; it's tough and durable and comes in a great assortment of colours, including ombré. If you want to invest in a crepe to get you started then this would be my top pick.

160g German - this is a nice durable crepe paper which comes in lots of bright intense colours. It is definitely worth having in your collection to experiment with and see how the paper works and moves using different techniques and mediums.
I suggest you start with a selection of yellows, whites and greens which will give you the basic colours to make most flowers.

WIRE

Florist stub wire or stem wire comes as flat lengths in different gauges (denoted by g). Gauge is a measure of thickness; the thinner the wire the larger the gauge. I like to have a couple of different thicknesses of stub wire in my kit bag. I use thin 26g for creeping climbers or smaller floppy flowers and thick 16g wire for flowers like roses and dahlias. Any wire between those two gauges, I refer to as medium thickness. In this book I will simply refer to thin, medium and thick wire, rather than gauges, to avoid complication.
Wire also comes in different lengths but you can always cut your strands of wire down to make them shorter or tape them together to lengthen them. You can also add tape or paper to make your wires thicker.
You can buy wires wrapped in green or white paper. I find paper-wrapped wire is really useful when you want to make fine stems. Green is useful for many projects but white is adaptable because it can be easily coloured using paints and ink. If you can't find paper-wrapped wire, you can colour any wire with a little acrylic paint.

GLUE
Hot glue is nice and strong and great for giving structure to larger flowers. However, it can be messy and hard to hide. I sometimes use hot glue to thicken stems or create knobbly bits. It can be easily covered with crepe paper when dry.

Tacky glue is where it's at! It is sticky, lightweight, dries quickly and a little goes a long way.

Mod Podge is an all-in-one glue, sealer, and finish designed for craft and art projects. The matte finish is perfect for most projects. It does come in lots of different finishes, including an antique finish which I love to use to give an aged look to petals and leaves.

PAPER CREASER
I have different shaped paper creasers for different jobs; I couldn't live without them. I find them especially useful for folding and manipulating small petals.

WIRE CUTTERS
Don't use scissors to cut your wire - they won't stay sharp for long if you do! Just get a pair of wire cutters or snips; they are inexpensive and you will use them lots.

A PENCIL
For marking and tracing.

FLORAL TAPE

Floral tape is made of crepe paper covered in a soft wax. It only sticks to itself but is soft and malleable and is great for thickening or sticking stems together or making bud shapes.

GREASEPROOF PAPER OR TRACING PAPER

I don't like to draw marks on the crepe paper so I always trace my templates onto greaseproof paper.

SCISSORS

I have big scissors to cut through thick stacks of crepe paper or to cut long strips from the roll. I have little scissors for fine details and I have my favourite sharp ones for making flowers that use a fringing technique. Fringing can be repetitive and strenuous on your hand so you may find spring loaded scissors are useful.

RULER

For measuring crepe and ribbons, and leaf, stamen and petal sizes.

LONG NOSE PLIERS

I have my rusty old faithful pliers at hand for bending thick wires.

TWEEZERS

Tweezers are handy for delicate work and handling tiny paper pieces.

PAINT BRUSHES, SPONGES, BLOTTERS, SOFT KNIVES AND APPLICATORS

These are some of the utensils needed to apply colour to your flowers.

FLOWER FROG

I use this lovely flower frog, kindly made for me by Louise Condon Designs, to hold my stems while I am building my flowers, but you could use a clamp or make some holes in a block of wood.

PALETTES, PLATES, BOWLS, OLD CUPS AND GLASSES

Vessels for paint, colour mixing, glue and water.

PAPER STRAWS

I find these handy to create thicker stems for flowers like tulips and dahlias.

AIR DRY CLAY

Non-toxic and easy to use, I sculpt seed pods and berries using a bit of air dry clay. It is easy to colour with a lick of paint.

CLAY TOOLS

Are great for making marks in the clay and sculpting and to get a nice smooth finish.

COLOURING

I love colouring my own paper. I get very excited when I talk about colouring and the different mediums I use! I don't have a favourite method of colouring and I urge you to try them all and experiment to find out what works best for you and your chosen flower.

Throughout the book I have tried to use lots of different colouring methods. I really enjoy mixing colours and applying them to paper to emulate the colours of nature. It's important to remember that different crepe papers act differently when they are coloured. I really like the way you don't always get an even look or the paper doesn't always absorb the colours evenly. To me, this adds to the authenticity of your flowers; nothing in nature is completely perfect.

WATER BASED PAINT AND INK

You can combine different colours of water based paints and inks together and dilute them with water to get the desired depth of colour or effect. Both of these mediums bleed and adhere to the paper nicely, dry quickly and can be applied with different tools. They are easy to apply smoothly and will bleed nicely into your paper to give the authentic colouration found in petals.

PASTELS

You cannot have enough pastels! There are so many to choose from and they offer such a wide range of colours. I recommend PanPastels - they come in a great assortment of colours, are lovely to use and you can mix them together easily.

TINTING

To obtain a very light delicate colour, you can soak a piece of coloured crepe in water.

The paper will colour the water creating a delicate tint. Some colours work better than others but have a play and see what works best for you.

I also like to rub a blob of glue or sealant into a piece of crepe with a brush. It will take on the colour, adding a light tint and finish.

WATER

I use water to drain the colour from my paper. Soaking paper in water reduces the paper colour. The longer you leave it in the water, the paler the colour will be.

ARTIST'S MARKER

Pens are becoming more readily available than ever thanks to the adult colouring book market.

Artist's markers are easy to use and you don't have all the cleaning up to do afterwards as you do with paint, brushes and palettes.

Alcohol, water or acrylic markers are available for different effects and in different nib sizes and shapes and a huge variety of colours. Markers can be applied quickly and easily to your paper to provide bold fade-resistant colour.

Alcohol markers are wonderful - they dry quickly, application is smooth, they bleed nicely and can be layered to

create great colours and effects. Watch out though, they can be smelly! Alcohol markers also blend well with water.

Acrylic pens are non-toxic and are fast drying; good for layering and blending to create more colours. It is better to pay a bit more for better quality acrylic pens, as they will contain less water and therefore have more vibrancy of colour.

Water based markers are inexpensive and widely available. However, on the downside, they come in a smaller range of colours and they do take longer to dry.

WATER COLOURS

Blocks of watercolour pigment are soluble in water, which means you can spread the colours with a sponge or brush.

Watercolours are translucent so they have a lovely bright colour which the light can shine through. They are perfect for creating a more delicate colouring effect.

BLEACH

Bleach is messy and smelly but used sparingly is great for taking the colour out of paper.

Wear gloves and a mask as bleach is an irritant. Be careful to handle your paper with care after bleaching as it can disintegrate if very fine or become brittle if you dip it in the bleach for too long.

COFFEE, TEA & NATURAL PIGMENTS

We are surrounded by natural pigments. I enjoy trying to experiment with natural pigments as often as I can. Not only is it a great way to use what is readily available to us in the natural world, but it keeps your

costs down too. Using natural pigments also means you are limiting the use of plastics and toxins so it is eco-friendly.

Using natural pigments is something I am keen to learn, experiment with and use more freely in my work in the future.

The earth is made up of rocks, clay and stone which all contain natural pigments. I am lucky to live in Yorkshire, which is an area rich in iron oxide which creates wonderful ochre colours.

Soot and charcoal can be used for greys and blacks.

Coffee and tea are my go-to natural products for creating brown pigments to age my paper leaves and petals.

Turmeric and saffron create wonderful rich yellow colours. Brambles, elderberries, hibiscus, marigolds, beetroot and red cabbage are all also great natural products to create a rainbow of colours.

CHALK

I use chalk to create pollen. I scrape coloured chalk with a knife to collect a fine powder. I then stick the chalk powder to the stamen with glue, and rub a little on the base of the petals where the pollen would naturally fall on a flower.

You can use pastels to create pollen but chalk gives a paler colour finish.

ACRYLIC PAINT

I use acrylic paint mainly for colouring clay. I like to layer up my colours for a more authentic natural look.

Inexpensive acrylic paints can be very thin and require a number of coats for full coverage so buy the best you can afford.

paper flower techniques

When it comes to paper flower making techniques, you will find the more time you practice manipulating your paper, the more lifelike your flowers will look. It is important that you never apply a petal cut direct from a roll of crepe paper; it must always have been subject to a manipulation technique first.

CUTTING RIBBONS

To make life a little easier, I like to cut my crepe paper roll into more manageable lengths, which I refer to as ribbons.

To make my ribbons, I unravel a 10" (25cm) length from the roll and cut a strip off along the grain. I then fold the strip in half and then half again and cut across the grain to create ribbons. These ribbons can now be coloured, outstretched, glued together, fringed or made into leaves or petals.

OUTSTRETCHING AND STRETCHING

I find when I am using a thicker paper it is easier to manipulate and gives a much more realistic finish if the paper is stretched or outstretched first. Once you have cut a ribbon of crepe the right length for the petals you are going to make, hold the paper at both ends and pull it gently, as if pulling apart. Some flowers may require you cut out the shape of the petal first and then stretch but the same method applies; just be gentle so you don't tear the paper. The heavier the paper the more it will stretch.

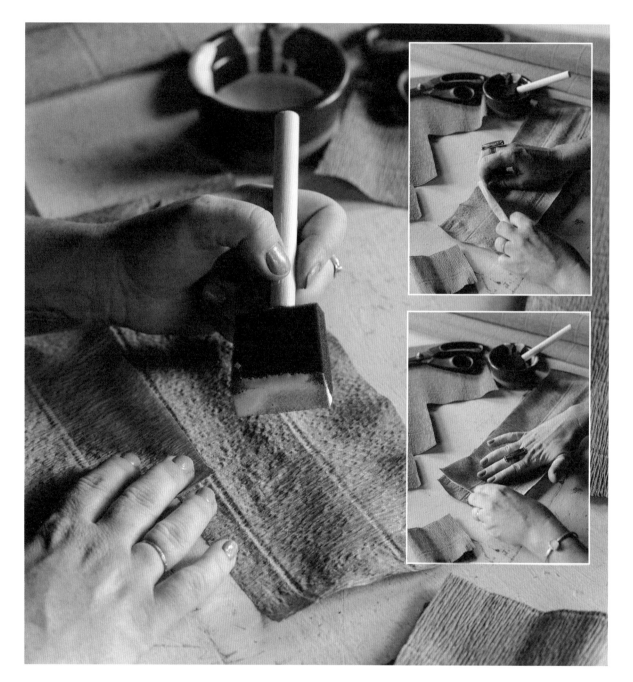

MAKING DOUBLE SIDED CREPE

This is great for flowers like roses that are a different colour on the top of the petal than the underneath, or leaves which are often different shades of green on either side.

Simply cut 2 ribbons of your chosen colours of crepe, outstretch both colours together and then apply an even layer of glue to one of the ribbons, stick the 2 ribbons together and allow them to dry.

TRACING AND CUTTING TEMPLATES

Each flower in the book has a set of templates for you to use to cut out your leaf and petal shapes. I trace the templates using tissue or baking paper and then use them to cut out my crepe paper shapes. I sometimes transfer my templates on to card, to give me a firmer template to draw around. Once you have your templates you can gauge the size of ribbons you need to cut from your crepe paper. Make your ribbons slightly larger than your templates. Check the instructions to see if you need to outstretch your paper before cutting out your templates. To save time you can fold your ribbons over to make 6 or 8 layers. Then you can cut out multiple petals at one time.

You need to cut along the grain so check which way the arrows on the templates are running before cutting your shapes.

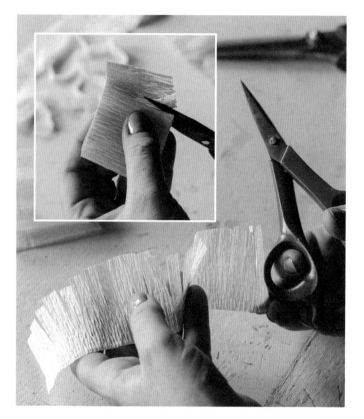

FRINGING

I use a fringing method to create stamens for the centre of my flowers.

First, you will need to cut a ribbon of paper across the grain of the height and width specified in the instructions.

If you are using thick crepe you may need to outstretch you paper for a finer finish. Alternatively, using a finer paper will give a finer fringing effect.

Fold the ribbon in half and then half again if the ribbon is long.

It is best to use small sharp scissors to cut your fringing. If you have them, spring loaded scissors can make the repetitive action easier on your hands.

Cut your fringing along the grain to the width stipulated in the flower instructions.

Try and leave ½" (1cm) or so unfringed so you can attach your fringing to your wire.

For more delicate flowers you may want to cut the excess paper from the base of the fringed strip. Do this by cutting small triangle shapes from the unfringed base of your paper.

To create thick fringing, I leave a wider gap between each cut. I then apply a thin layer of tacky glue and roll each piece of fringing between my thumb and finger to create a much thicker fringe. I use this method when making verrone's obsidian dahlia and echinacea pallida.

CURLING

Curling finishes the edges of petals and leaves. I use a different thickness of tool depending on the finish I want to achieve. Good tools for curling are knitting needles, skewers, thick stub wire, hat pins and even toothpicks for tiny leaves and petals, Fold the edge you want to curl around the tool and wind either under or over the tool depending on the direction you want your paper to curl.

FLUTING

This method of manipulation will add ruffles to the edges of petals. To create ruffles you need to start by stretching the crepe slightly across the grain. Place the paper between your thumbs and forefingers and move the paper in the opposite direction as if tearing the paper in half. Move along the edge of the petal and repeat this technique, placing your thumb and forefinger in the ruffle you have made previously.

CUPPING AND REVERSE CUPPING

This technique shapes the paper into a cup-like shape. Put your thumbs in the middle of the top of the petal shape and your forefingers on the opposite side and gently push your thumbs away and out to create the cup shape.

For reverse cupping, use the same method on the bottom of the petal. You can also curl the edges of your paper by moving your thumbs and fingers towards the top of the petal so the paper curls over your thumbs.

BASE OF PETAL FOLDING, PINCHING AND TWISTING

All 3 of these manipulation techniques help to shape the petal and strengthen the structure of your flower.

Pinching the base of the petal together and securing it with a little tacky glue can add to the natural cupped shape of some petals. It can also help narrow the petal shape towards the base where it attaches to the stem and gives a more rigid form to the flower. You can also do this to the back of the petal as you will notice that some flowers have petals that naturally fall backwards in the opposite direction to the cup. Have a look at the most outward petals of a rose for a good example.

MAKING LEAVES

I find the best way to make leaves is to cut a ribbon of crepe and colour or laminate 2 colours together to create a ribbon with a different coloured top and underside. Once I have made my ribbon I fold it in half multiple times until I have a square the approximate size of the leaf I am going to make. For the most realistic looking leaves you ideally want the grain of the paper to run the same way as the veins in a leaf. To achieve this, you will need to fold your squares of folded paper in half on the diagonal. You will then have a straight fold line to cut along.

When you unfold the paper the triangles you have created will need separating. I promise this will make more sense when you

are making leaves.

For each leaf you will need 2 triangles with the paper grain running from the bottom of the leaf upwards and outwards, like that of a natural leaf vein. Make sure the same coloured side of the paper is facing the right way too.

For each leaf you need to cut the left and right sides using your templates.

Once you have the 2 sides of your leaf, put a line of tacky glue down the central line of both sides. Next choose a piece of wire. The thickness of wire you choose will depend on the size and structure of the leaf you are making - a small delicate leaf will require a thinner wire than a bigger leaf for instance. Place the wire along the glue line of one of your leaves, making sure you don't stick it

quite all the way to the top of the leaf. Apply more glue along the wire and then place the other side of the leaf on top of it and press down firmly. I like to run a paper creaser down each side to add definition to the central vein made by the wire. It also helps to make sure that the paper and wire are stuck firmly together. Using the template, cut the leaf shape out.

You can now add brown edges or age your leaves with a little splodge of coffee or tea, before letting it dry.

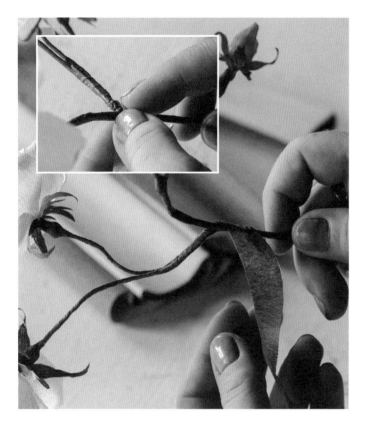

ATTACHING FLOWERS AND LEAVES TO STEMS

Some flowers, especially tall flowers such as larkspur, have 1 stem with multiple flowers. These flowers all need attaching to the stem. First, I make my stem using the correct length of wire and attach any buds at the top with floral tape.

Next I thicken the stem by wrapping floral tape all the way down it's length. If you look at real flower you will see that stems are almost always thicker at the base and thinner at the top, so emulate that for a realistic look.

Finally, I cut ribbons of the colour of crepe I am using for the stem. I outstretch my ribbon, apply glue to it and then, starting from the top of the stem, attach the flowers and leaves in their natural pattern of growth, using the glued crepe as a tape.

To attach large, heavy flower heads and leaves to stems you may find using a piece of floral tape first helps provide extra strength.

FINISHING YOUR FLOWERS

You will notice some flowers are matte, some are glossy and some have matte petals but glossy leaves and stems. To create my desired finish, I use a matte or gloss sealant applied with a brush.

UV protection sprays are available to buy to help preserve your flowers from fading. You can also buy pastel protection sprays, which you can use as you work for a faster application of multiple flowers or stems.

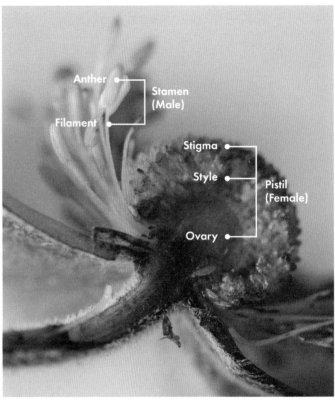

THE BASIC ANATOMY OF A FLOWER

It is useful to have a basic understanding of the anatomy of flower before you start paper flower making. Flowers are complex and made up of many different elements but here are the most commonly parts of a flower.

Petals - these give the flower its shape and colour and are designed to attract insects.

Pistil (stigma/style/ovary) - this is the female part of the flower. The **style** is the stalk part of the pistil and the **stigma** is the area which would receive the pollen in the process of fertilization. You cannot see the **ovary** but it is found at the very base in the centre of the flower.

Calyx - is found at the top of the stem at the base of the petals and is made up of sepals.

Sepals - are leaf-like and protect the flower when it is in bud. The base of the flower where the sepals are attached is where the flower's main organs are contained. You don't need to know what these look like for flower making, but it's wonderful to marvel at what fabulous creations flowers are and wonder at what nature has blessed us with.

Stamen - the male part of the flower, consists of 2 parts, the **anther** and the **filament.** The filament is the stalk that holds up the anther. The anther produces pollen.

Stem - also called a **peduncle** or **stalk**. A flower head is attached to the stem along with its leaves. A stem is there to support the flower and transport nutrients from the ground to the flower and leaves.

the flowers

For a floral artist - be it painter, maker or florist - flowers bring such joy. From the bright yellow daffodils of spring, to the colourful scented blooms of summer, the fruits and ferns of autumn to the cones, berries and greenery of winter, every season is filled with inspiration. I hope you will be inspired by these projects to get creative and make your own fabulous paper flowers.

poppy

Poppies come in single and double forms and in an array of bright colours. Throughout the summer months, their flower heads can be seen nodding on the end of their tall slender stems in cornfields and along roadside verges. Easy to grow, they are a gardener's favourite.

What you'll need

- Essential kit bag
- White crepe paper
- Green crepe paper
- Yellow/orange marker
- Air dry clay
- Crafting knife
- Acrylic paint - greens
- Yellow chalk powder

See page 134 for templates

With their tissue paper like petals how could I not include the simple elegant poppy?

I chose to put this beautiful flower at the beginning of the book as poppies have a relatively simple structure. Poppies have a thin stem and no calyx, so you can experiment a bit with paper thicknesses to make the petals. You can also try working with different colours and mediums to get a feel for the effect they have on your paper.

Fig. 1.

Fig. 2.

HOW TO MAKE A SINGLE POPPY

1. Cut a ribbon of white crepe paper 15-23cm (6-9") long and 2.5cm (1") wide for each poppy.

2. Colour along the length of one edge with orange/yellow marker.

3. Fringe along the coloured length and set your pieces aside.

4. Cut an 8cm (3") lengths of crepe.

5. Outstretch the ribbon and fold it in half and then half again

Making the petals

6. Using petal No. 1 template, cut out 2 petals per poppy.

7. Using petal No. 2 template, cut 2 petals out per poppy.

8. Crumple the petals up tightly

9. Un-crumple the petals and stack them in their sizes

Making the seed pod

10. Take a small piece of air dry clay. It should be a little larger than pea-sized

11. Form the clay into a ball, using the seed pod template as a size guide. Make a hook from a medium piece of stub wire and push into the clay ball to make your stem.

12. Gently roll the ball in between your thumb and finger to create an oval shape

13. (Fig. 1.) Using a sharp knife cut off the top of the oval shape to create the disk shape on the top of the poppy seed head.

Fig. 3.

Fig. 4.

Use the tip of a knife to make lines running from the centre of the seed head to the outer edges to create the characteristic markings.

14. Allow the clay seed head to dry.

15. Paint it with some green acrylic paint.

16. The paint should pool in the lines and emphasise them. If you want to make them darker, add a slightly darker shade. Allow the seed head to dry.

Making the stamen

17. (Fig. 2.) Apply glue to the base of the fringed crepe and wrap it around the stem, just under the clay seed head, to form the stamen.

18. Dip the stamen a little glue and yellow chalk dust to create a pollen effect.

Assembling the finished stem

19. Take 2 of each of the different sized petals and gently cup.

20. Rub a little yellow chalk dust in the centre of cup shape.

21. Add tacky glue to the petal bases.

22. (Fig. 3.) Take the 2 petal No. 1 template petals and glue to the stem, underneath the stamen, so they sit opposite each other.

23. Take 2 of the petal No. 2 template petals and glue in the gaps, so they sit behind the first petals.

24. (Fig. 4.) Cut a ribbon of green crepe and, starting at the base of the flowers wrap it around the stem, until you reach the end of the wire. Make sure you completely cover where the petals meet the stem.

evening primrose, 'apricot delight'

Evening Primrose always catches my eye where ever I see it growing. It is a night flowering plant and the Apricot Delight variety has the most beautiful colouration which varies from soft lemon yellow to apricot to salmon pink, depending on the plant and the age of the flowers.

What you'll need

- ▪ Essential kit bag
- ▪ Crepe paper
- ▪ Paints, inks, markers, pastels
- ▪ Colours to consider for both paper and mediums are green, maroon, dark red, lemon yellow, various shade of orange and pink

See page 134 for templates

I just love everything about Evening Primrose. It was especially appealing to me to make in paper as it only opens at night so it makes a terrible cut flower. You can enjoy an Evening Primrose paper flower at any time of the day or night.

The whole of the Evening Primrose is edible, but the plant is most well-known for its oil, which has many health benefits.

Fig. 1.

Fig. 2.

HOW TO MAKE EVENING PRIMROSE 'APRICOT DELIGHT'

Making the stems

1. (Fig. 1.) Take a thick piece of stub wire and a slightly thinner piece and tape them together using floral tape to form a stem that should measure approximately 60cm (24"). Keep wrapping tape around the base to make it thicker.

Making the pistils and stamens

3. (Fig. 2.) Cut ribbons of yellow crepe paper approx 1cm (½") thick. Apply tacky glue along the length of the ribbon and roll it up to form a string of crepe. Once dry you need to cut it into 3 different lengths. For each flower you need to cut a piece measuring 7.5cm (3") for the pistil in the centre and 5 x 4cm (1½") and 5 x 1cm (½") lengths for the stamen of each rose. Use the stamen template as a size guide. Glue the end of the 7.5cm (3") piece of crepe string and allow to dry.

4. (Fig. 3.) Glue each of your 1cm (½") pieces to the top of each of your 4cm (1½") pieces to form a T-shape and allow all 5 to dry.

5. Make some pollen using yellow chalk.

6. Dip the T-shapes in tacky glue and then the chalk pollen and allow them to dry.

7. Carefully split the top of the central pistil into 4 even strands and gently curl each strand outwards using a length of thick wire.

8. (Fig. 4.) Carefully hot glue the 5

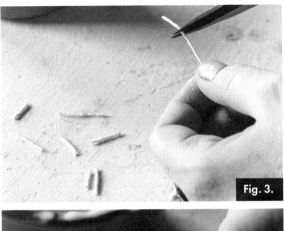

Fig. 3.

Fig. 4.

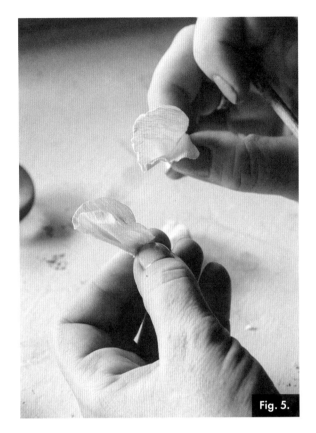

Fig. 5.

T-shaped stamens around the pistil.

Making the petals

2. For the petals, choose the crepe you would like to use. Cut lengths of ribbon measuring 7.5cm (3") across the paper grain and colour with lemon yellow, apricot and salmon pink colours. I used a fine crepe with watercolour pens and pastels.

9. Take your coloured crepe paper and fold over on itself 4 times.

10. Cut the petals out using the template.

11. Very slightly cup each petal and fold the petal edges back gently over a skewer.

12. (Fig. 5.) Apply a little tacky glue to the petal base and pinch the base together. Do this with all four petals.

13. Place all four petals evenly around the stamen.

Making the sepals

14. (Fig. 6.) Cut some 7.5cm (3") length ribbons of crepe and colour using a maroon medium of your choice. I used an artist's maker pen.

15. Using the template cut out 4 sepal shapes.

16. (Fig. 7.) Apply tacky glue to the bottom of your sepals and attach to the base of each petal.

17. Use floral tape to create a shape that is thicker at the top than the bottom, where it will be attached to the main stem. Add a strip of the green/maroon ribbon by tacky

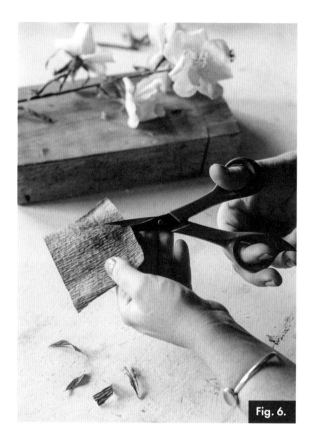

Fig. 6.

Fig. 7.

gluing the ribbon and twisting it around to cover the floral tape.

Making spent buds

18. Spent buds can be made using thin wire wrapped with floral tape to create the correct thickness and shape. Use the bud template as a size guide.

19. Cover the floral tape with a ribbon of green/maroon crepe and press a skewer or the end of your scissors into the top to create a dent.

Repeat the process to make between 4 to 8 flowers per stem.

Making the leaves

20. Cut leaves from the green/maroon crepe. These will be fixed at the base of each flower and each spent bud. Start attaching the flowers and a leaf approximately 5cm (2") from the main stem. Rotate your stem as you add the flowers so they are attached evenly around the stem. Secure them by wrapping with a little floral tape.

Assembling the finished stem

21. Place a few spent buds and leaves at the base of the main stem.

22. (Fig. 8.) Wrap the whole stem in a length of green/maroon crepe ribbon to cover where you have attached all the flower buds and leaves, Make as many stems as you need and finish with a sealant.

Twisting the stem as you add your flowers and spent buds ensures your twigs look natural and even. I love these prettily displayed in vases on my kitchen table or hall table.

Fig. 8.

floribunda rose

I love to grow a Floribunda Rose in my garden for its dramatic colour. When I go into the garden it immediately catches my eye and I just adore its wavy edged petals. The beautiful tangerine and peachy pink ruffles make a great statement piece and add a lovely splash of colour to any room.

What you'll need

- Essential kit bag
- Crepe paper in orange and pink shades
- Yellow and brown chalk powder
- Light brown marker
- Paints, inks, markers, pastels in oranges and pinks

See page 135 for templates

I chose this variety of rose for its unusual petal shape and its beautiful colouration.

Floribunda or 'Easy Does It' is a fairly new variety of rose. Its irregular shaped petals give it the unusual ruffled look. With its masses of soft apricot fading to pink blooms and waxy dark green leaves, it is a real head-turner.

Fig. 1.

Fig. 2.

HOW TO MAKE FLORIBUNDA ROSE

1. (Fig. 1.) Start with the stamens. Cut ribbons just over 2.5cm (1") tall from yellow/gold crepe.

2. Outstretch the ribbons and cut into approximately 20cm (8") lengths.

3. Colour along one long edge with light brown paint, pen or pastel.

4. Fringe the ribbon.

5. Curl a thick piece of stub wire into a hook shape with a pair of long nose pliers.

6. Put tacky glue along the base of the ribbon on opposite side to the light brown coloured edge.

7. Wrap the ribbon over the wire hook so no wire is showing. This will provide stability to your flower.

8. Dip in glue and a little mix of brown and yellow chalk powder.

9. Colour or use ready-coloured crepe in orange and peachy pink shades.

Making the petals

10. (Fig. 2.) Cut the templates for each size of petal (6 of No.1, 10 of No.2, 14 of No.3) and stack them in their sizes.

11. (Fig. 3.) Shade all of the petals using soft pastels in yellow/orange/pink shades.

12. (Fig. 4. 5. and 6.) Cup and curl the smallest No. 1 petals inwards, add tacky glue, pinch their bases and randomly add them around the stamen.

Floribunda Roses
are prized for creating
a mass of colour by
bearing many flowers
in large clusters over
a long season.

Fig. 3.

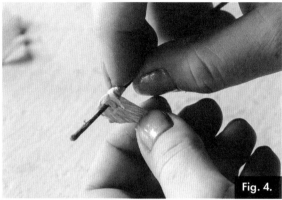

Fig. 4.

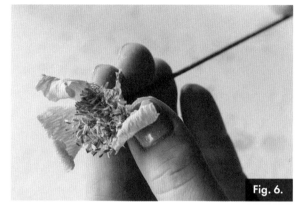

Fig. 6.

Fig. 5.

Fig. 7.

13. Cup the No.2 petals and curl some of the edges in and some out. Tacky glue and pinch the bases and stick them evenly around the No.1 petals.

14. Reverse cup the No.3 petals and curl the edges outwards. Tacky glue and pinch the bases in and arrange the petals evenly around the No.2 petals.

Making the sepals

15. (Fig. 7.) Cut 5 sepals using the template. Gently cup the wider part of each sepal and glue around the base of the petals at the back of the flower, leaving no gaps.

16. Curl each sepal with thick stub wire at its edges and add a little brown or maroon colour to the tips or edges if you like.

Assembling the finished stem

17. Wrap a small length of floral tape around the wire at the bottom of the sepals to create a small bulb shape. This will form the base of the calyx.

18. Wrap the stem in floral tape to the required thickness.

19. Cut 30cm (12") ribbons from green crepe, apply tacky glue and use to finish the stem.

20. Add leaves if you desire using the leaf templates and leaf pattern provided Attach securely to the stem with green crepe ribbon.

geum, 'mai tai'

Geum 'Mai Tai' has branching, red-green stems on which pink-flushed, apricot flowers appear from late spring to summer. I have chosen this delicate little flower because I love its frilly semi-double petals and its long stems which make them ideal for cutting.

What you'll need

■ Essential kit bag

■ Crepe paper

■ Orange marker

■ Brown marker

■ Paints, pastels or inks in peach, caffe latte, apricot, lime green, leaf green

See page 135 for templates

Geum plants produce single, double and semi double flower heads. Commonly known as Avens, these little flowers bloom from late spring until early autumn.

Look for other varieties like 'Custard Tart', 'Totally Tangerine' and 'Scarlet Tempest', which all produce pretty coloured blooms, perfect for paper flowers.

Fig. 1.

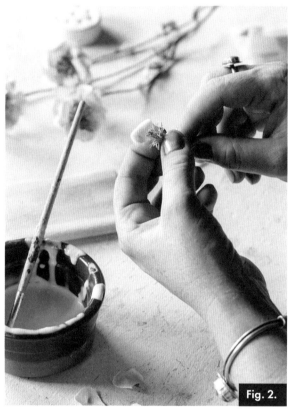

Fig. 2.

HOW TO MAKE GEUM, 'MAI TAI'

1. Cut ribbons of lime green crepe 2.5cm (1") in length and colour along the top edge with orange.

2. Cut another slightly taller ribbon from yellow crepe and colour along the top with patches of brown.

3. Finely fringe both ribbons, starting with the orange and brown coloured lines. This will form the top of the stamen.

4. Curve a piece of thin stub wire to form a hook shape at the top.

5. Tacky glue the bottom of the strip of lime green crepe and attach over the hook to conceal the wire.

6. Glue the bottom edge of the yellow ribbon and wrap evenly around the green.

Making the petals

7. Choose your crepe paper. Peachy apricots are best for Mai Tai. Here I have chosen a fine crepe and coloured a large piece with orange watercolours and left it to dry.

8. Cut 2.5cm (1") ribbons from the crepe and fold into 8 and cut out 2-3 x No.1 and 9 x No.2 petals using the templates. .

9. (Fig. 1.) Add a little extra colour to the petals if desired.

10. Gently cup each tiny petal. As the petals are so small and delicate I like to use the end of a small paint brush to gently rub the centre of the petal with small circular motions. This gently curls the petal upwards

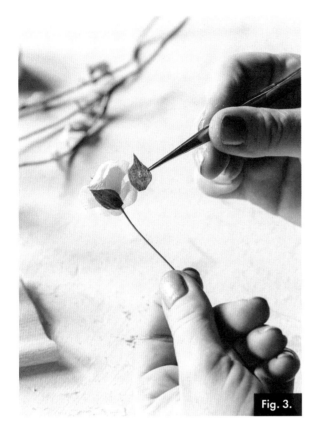

Fig. 3.

Fig. 4.

and forms a tiny bowl shape.

11. Use a thick piece of stub wire to curl the top edges of each No.1 petal inward as if they are unfurling.

12. (Fig. 2.) Apply a tiny bit of tacky glue around the fringed centre and add the petals. I like to overlap 3 petals and then fill the gap with a fourth. Move carefully around the flower building a nice even shape. Add 2-3 x No.1 petals to some of the flowers to create a few semi-double flower heads.

Making the sepals

13. Cut some ribbons of green crepe approx 2.5cm (1") and colour in patches in shades of red and brown.

14. Cut 5 sepals per flower from the coloured green ribbons using the template.

15. (Fig. 3.) Attach 1 at 12 o'clock one at 5 o'clock and 1 at 7 o'clock. Put the remaining 2 sepals in the gaps at approximately 10 and 2 o'clock.

Making the leaves

16. Cut leaf shapes from the green crepe.

Assembling the finished stem

17. (Fig. 4.) Glue a strip of the green coloured ribbon and wrap it round the stem from the base of the sepals downwards, tucking in some of your tiny leaf shapes intermittently as you go, with larger leaves at the base of the stem.

dahlia 'verrone's obsidian'

Dahlias were originally imported for their tubers, which were eaten as a potato substitute! Dark and sultry, the inward rolled petals look as if they have been cut from the deepest maroon-black silk velvet. With their bright contrasting sun-burst eyes, bees will be drawn to them in any garden.

What you'll need

- Essential kit bag
- Crepe paper in black and leaf green
- Glossy glue
- Orange chalk powder
- Yellow chalk powder
- Pastels in red, pink, purple
- Applicator for pastel

See page 136 for templates

Dahlias are said to be symbolic of elegance and good taste. Their inward curling petals give them an unusual and eye catching structure and they often come in gorgeous burnt sienna and orange colour ways.

If you enjoyed making this flower, try making the 'Honka Fragile' Dahlia, which is star shaped and delicate in hue.

Fig. 1.

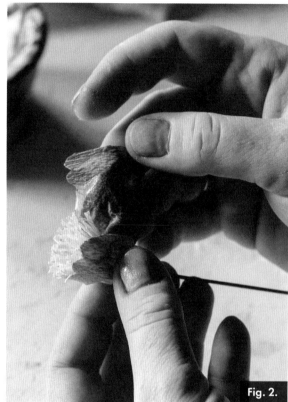

Fig. 2.

HOW TO MAKE DAHLIA, 'VERRONE'S OBSIDIAN'

Making the disc floret (Fig. 1.)

1. Disc florets are the small tubular flowers at the centre of the flower head. Start by making a hook at the top of a thick length of stub wire.

2. To make the disc floret, cut a 2.5cm (1") tall by 10cm (4") wide ribbon from orange/yellow crepe. Outstretch and thick fringe your ribbons.

3. Glue along the fringed edge and gently roll the separate fringes between your thumb and forefinger to make the thick tubular shaped florets.

4. Apply glue along the base and wrap over the hook, concealing the wire.

5. Apply a little glue and some orange and yellow chalk powder.

6. Next make slightly thinner fringed ribbons, dip in glue and orange and yellow chalk powder. This is for the thinner outer part of the disc floret.

7. Glue the base of the fringing and wrap it around the thicker part of the disc floret in the centre.

Making the bracts (Fig.2.)

8. The florets of this dahlia are held together by bracts. Using the templates provided, cut the bracts (approx 8 per flower) from out stretched pale green crepe and gently cup each section to give a little shape. Dab with a little glossy glue and wrap around the

54

Fig. 3.

Fig. 4.

central florets.

9. Glossy glue the outer side of the bracts and allow them to dry.

Making the petals

10. Cut ribbons of 10cm (4") tall black crepe. Overstretch but not too much. Cut out 8 petals per flower using the template.

11. Slightly cup the widest part near the base of the petal.

12. (Fig. 3.) Colour each petal with soft pastels and a sponge applicator or brush. Use red towards the petal base and purple shades towards the tip.

13. (Fig. 4.) Using the lines on the template, fold the petal over and run a paper creaser or your nail along the fold

14. Using a skewer roll both sides of the petal in towards the centre.

15. Roll the tip of the petal over backwards slightly.

16. Spray with a little pastel sealant and allow to dry.

17. Apply a small amount of tacky glue to the base of the petal.

18. Carefully fold both sides of the base inwards slightly to force the petal to curl inwards, giving it its glorious shape.

19. Apply tacky glue and add the petals evenly around the base of the bract.

20. Once the glue has dried, carefully bend the petal back at the base towards the stem.

21. Wrap a couple of layers of floral tape around the petal.

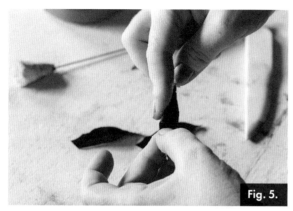

Fig. 5.

Fig. 6.

Fig. 7.

Making the phyllaries

22. Cut 8 phyllaries using the template from outstretched heavy, light green crepe.

23. Cup and then crease down the centre.

24. Attach them behind the petals so they cover the back of the petal by 1cm (½").

25. Wrap a thin ribbon in the same colour around the base of the sepals to cover any glue and gaps.

26. Smooth the ribbon and the backs of the phyllaries with a brush and some glossy glue and allow to dry.

27. At the base of the phyllaries smaller leaf-like structures face in the opposite direction. Using the template, cut them from the same green crepe.

28. (Fig. 7.) Apply tacky glue to the base and stick to the base of the flower head where it joins the stem.

29. (Fig. 8.) Once dry, bend these little leaf shapes backwards towards the stem.

Making the leaves

30. Make leaves using the leaf template.

Assembling the finished stem

31. Wrap floral tape around the stem until it is thick enough. Stick dark green crepe around the stem, adding a couple of leaves half way down.

32. Add a little maroon colouring to the stem leaving the top 7.5cm (3") nearest the flower head green.

Phyllaries are leaf-like structures that form one or more whorls immediately below a flower head. In dahlias they do the same job as sepals and bracts in other flowers.

Fig. 8.

rowan berries, 'sorbus aucuparia'

I love this tree so much that I gave my youngest son the name Rowan as his middle name. In the autumn, Rowan trees are full of clusters of beautiful berries. Different varieties have different coloured berries and, even when the leaves fall, they are left hanging brightly for the birds.

What you'll need

■ Essential kit bag

■ Air dry clay

■ Acrylic paint in rusts, reds, brown

■ Crepe paper in green and brown

■ Craft knife

See page 136 for templates

I wanted to include Rowan in the book for something a little different. In floristry, I often forage for fruits and berries to include in my arrangements; they give shape and texture to a design. The distinctive leaves of the Rowan tree are perfect for paper flower making.

I hope making this Rowan will give you the confidence to make other fruits and berries from clay and paper.

Fig. 1.

Fig. 2.

Fig. 3.

HOW TO MAKE ROWAN BERRIES, 'SORBUS AUCUPARIA'

Making the berries

1. Hook pieces of 7.5cm (3") long thin wire

2. (Fig. 1.) Roll small lumps of clay into balls. Use the berry template as a size guide.

3. Pierce through the clay balls with the hook to form a stalk.

4. (Fig. 2.) Make a 5 point star shape on the top of each berry, using a sharp knife. Use the berry template for guidance.

5. Allow the clay to dry fully.

6. (Fig. 3.) Paint your berries with your choice of acrylic paint colour.

7. Once dry, paint the star shape with a brown/black colour.

Assembling the finished stem

8. Join your wires together to form bunches of five berries and attach to medium thick stub wire with floral tape.

9. Cut out the leaf shapes and attach them individually to a medium thick piece of stub wire with a ribbon of brown crepe paper or brown floral tape.

10. Take a piece of thick stub wire and bend slightly, start with a bunch of the berries and attach to the end of the wire with brown floral tape until you are happy with the look.

11. Add your leaves.

12. (Fig. 4.) Thicken the wire with tape.

Cover your stems with ribbons of coloured crepe if you want to create a weathered moss or bark effect.

Fig. 4.

hybrid musk rose, 'rosa kew gardens'

'Rosa Kew Gardens' is such a charming and graceful rose with a delicate musk fragrance. It's a thorn-free shrub rose which bears a profusion of small, single white flowers with pretty soft apricot centres all through summer. I love how the buds are yellow before they burst into white flowers.

What you'll need

- Essential kit bag
- Crepe paper in cream, white, yellow and green
- Brown marker
- Orange marker
- Yellow pastel

See page 137 for templates

I really had to include an English rose in the book and I could think of nothing nicer than this delicate little shrub.

It is made up of single white pollen rich flowers, which gives them their pretty yellow centres. 'Rosa Kew Gardens' can have multiple flowers per head so you can keep it simple or add lots of flowers.

HOW TO MAKE HYBRID MUSK ROSE, 'ROSA KEW GARDENS'

Making the flower centre and stamen

1. Hook a medium thick piece of stub wire.

2. Cut 1cm (½") ribbons of crepe - pale yellow for older flowers and bright yellow for newer flowers.

3. Fringe the ribbons.

4. Colour the top edge of the paler yellow ribbons with a brown pen. Colour the brighter yellow ribbons with an orange pen.

5. (Fig. 1.) Tacky glue the base of the fringed ribbon and wrap it over the hook, completely covering the wire.

Making the petals

6. Cut petals for the younger flowers from cream crepe, using the young petal template. For the older flowers, use white crepe and the older petals templates. Rub a little yellow pastel at the bases of the younger cream flower petals.

7. Cup the petals.

8. Tacky glue the bases and pinch together.

9. (Fig. 2.) Apply a little glue at the bases of the flowers and add the fringing, overlapping here and there.

Making the sepals

10. Cut the sepals from outstretched green crepe, using the sepal template.

11. Tacky glue their bases and attach evenly behind each flower at the base of the petals.

Assembling the finished stem

12. (Fig. 3.) With floral tape, make small ball shapes at the base of each flower.

13. (Fig. 4.) Cut ribbons of green crepe and glue them around the stem from top to bottom.

14. Attach more flowers and leaves using floral tape or a ribbon of green crepe.

Fig. 4.

cherry blossom 'kanzan'

Cherry blossom trees originate in Japan and are renowned for their beautiful display of flowers. Different varieties produce single, double or semi-double blooms in pinks and white. Cherry blossom adds a different texture and variety to a display or bouquet.

What you'll need

- Essential kit bag
- Crepe paper in white and various shades of pink, green, grey and brown
- Paints, pastels or inks in maroon, brown, pinks and greens

See page 137 for templates

This beautiful Japanese Cherry Blossom is incredibly striking in the spring, with its plumes of luscious double, intense pink blooms, followed by stunning bronze foliage.

This flower is one of my absolute favourites to make and worth taking your time over - it can be a little tricky, with its multiple flower heads and tiny petals, but it is well worth it.

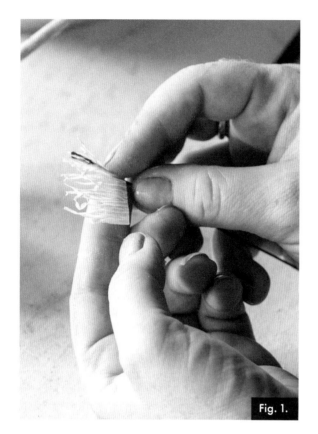

Fig. 1.

Fig. 2.

HOW TO MAKE CHERRY BLOSSOM 'KANZAN'

Preparation

1. Fringe 2.5cm x 2.5cm (1" x 1") ribbons of white crepe paper.

2. Cut the fringed ribbons into 1cm (½") lengths. You will need approximately 20 ribbons to make the number of flowers on the stem pictured.

3. (Fig. 1.) Glue and wrap the ribbons around 10cm (4") lengths of thin stub wire.

4. Cut 2.5cm (1")   ribbons of white and pink crepe.

Making the petals

5. (Fig. 2.) Outstretch and cut out No.1 petal temples. You need 4-6 per flower head.

6. (Fig. 3.) Place the petals evenly around the fringed centre.

7. Cut 5cm (2") ribbons from a mix of different pink crepes and colour if desired.

8. Using No.2 petal template, cut 10-14 petals per flower. I like to make a bunch and mix the different pinks.

9. Cut 10 petals from No.3 petal template. Cup and curl these petals.

Making the sepals (Fig. 4.)

10. Colour 2.5cm (1") ribbons of green crepe with a little maroon or red medium.

11. Cut 5 sepals for each flower from this crepe, using the sepal template.

12. Glue to the back of the flowers.

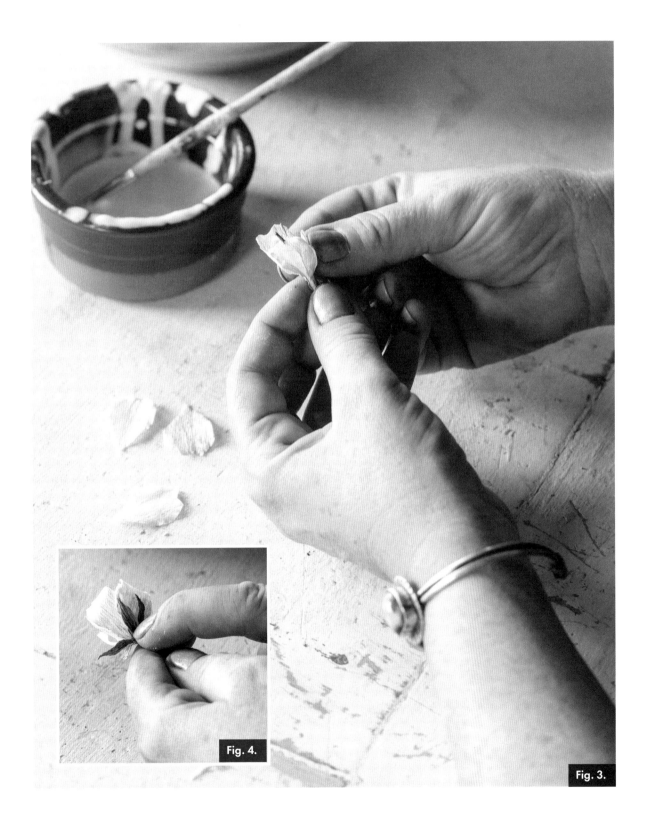

Fig. 4.

Fig. 3.

Fig. 5.

Fig. 6.

Making the leaves

13. Make as many leaves as you like. You can use coloured green crepe or a lovely bronze or copper would work really well.

Assembling the finished stem

14. (Fig. 5.) Wrap the stems of the flowers and the leaves together using ribbons of coloured green crepe.

15. Make bunches of 4-6 flowers and attach them with floral tape to thick stub wire.

16. (Fig. 6.) Wrap over the tape with ribbons of coloured green crepe paper.

17. If you want to add leaves, attach the smaller ones to the top of a thick length thick stub wire, using floral tape. This will form the main branch for the flowers to sit on.

18. Add two larger leaves a couple of inches below the small leaves.

19. Now start adding the bunches of blossom alternately either side of the stem, attaching with floral tape as you go along.

20. Once all the blossom bunches are attached, use the floral tape to thicken the base of the stem.

21. (Fig. 7.) Cover the floral tape with ribbons of crepe. I used coloured green crepe at the top of the stem, merging into grey/brown crepe for the bark.

The bark of the Cherry Blossom 'Kanzan' starts reddish brown and later turns brownish grey and furrowed. Use different colours of brown and maroon crepe to create this distinctive look.

Fig. 7.

hydrangea paniculata, 'limelight'

I love this hydrangea! Its unusual eye-catching, cone-shaped mound of dense little flowers starts out an acid green colour, before the flowers open into ivory that become washed in pink with age. This is an incredibly hardy shrub for the garden, which I cut and use frequently in large displays.

What you'll need

- Essential kit bag
- Crepe paper in cream and green
- Paints, pastels or inks in greens and pinks

See page 138 for templates

This is my favourite of all the hydrangeas. The tiny flowers with their tones of green, cream and pink give it a beautiful three-toned effect. Since each flower head looks like a mini bouquet, they stand alone in a vase beautifully, or their big blowzy heads fill arrangements out quickly .

Fig. 1.

Fig. 2.

Fig. 3.

HOW TO MAKE HYDRANGEA PANICULATA 'LIMELIGHT'

Making the petals

1. (Fig. 1.) Colour cream or palest green crepe with shades of pink and green.
2. Using the templates, cut lots of tiny petals from the coloured crepe and put aside.

Making the flower centres

3. Cut 10cm (4") lengths from thin white wire, which has been paper wrapped or painted.
4. Bend over the tips of the wires to make tiny hoops. This will form the centres of each flower.
5. Put glue on 3-4 of the petal bases and attach them around the wire hoops.

Making the Hydrangea heads

6. Dab the stems with green paint or marker.
7. (Fig. 2.) Take individual flowers and group into bunches of 5, wrapping them together with floral tape. You will need 10 bunches for each hydrangea head.
8. Cut ribbons of green crepe and tacky glue them, ready to secure the flower heads to the wire.
9. (Fig. 3.) Take a thick length of stub wire and attach one of the bunches right at the end, keeping the stems of the bunch short.
10. To make the conical shape of the hydrangea head you need to increase the stem length of each flower head as you descend down the main stem.

Fig. 4.

Making the leaves

11. Make some leaves using the leaf templates. Attach smaller leaves at the top and larger leaves at the base of the stem.

Assembling the finished stem

12. (Fig. 4.) Finish your flower head by wrapping ribbons of green crepe down the length of the main stem to the desired thickness.

echinacea pallida, 'pale purple coneflower'

Also called the purple coneflower, this herbaceous perennial is native to the North American prairies, but I grow them in my garden in Yorkshire. I love their tall stems and the way their long slender petals fall downwards. Used for medicinal purposes, Echinacea also makes wonderful cut flowers.

What you'll need

- ▨ Essential kit bag
- ▨ Crepe paper in brown, green and white
- ▨ Pastels in orange and pink
- ▨ Paints and inks in pinks and purples

See page 138 for templates

I have chosen the coneflower because its minimal simplicity makes the most wonderful display - just one stem in a glass bottle will draw your eye.

The tall flower with its orangey-brown centre and slender pale purple and pink petals give it such a distinctive look.

Fig. 1.

Fig. 2.

HOW TO MAKE ECHINACEA PALLIDA 'PALE PURPLE CONEFLOWER'

1. Cut 2 x 3.5cm x 25cm (1½" x 10") ribbons from brown crepe and outstretch.

2. Colour with oranges and pinks.

3. Thick fringe and apply tacky glue.

4. Roll each piece of thick fringing to create the spikes that make up the cone shape at the centre, and allow to dry.

5. Make a hook 2.5cm (1") from the top of a thick piece of stub wire using long nose pliers. Then attach another length of thick stub wire using floral tape to make a stem approximately 55cm (22") long.

6. Cover the hook with floral tape, creating a bulb shape around the cone.

7. Wrap the tape up and down the stem.

8. Tacky glue along the unfringed edge of the coloured brown crepe.

9. Glue one end of the fringed ribbon at the top of the centre of the bulb shape.

10. (Fig. 1.) Keep wrapping the fringed ribbon round and round until the bulb shape is covered, forming the central cone shape.

Making the petals

11. Colour some white or cream crepe paper with paints or inks in dark pink or purple. Echinacea petals are long, so check the templates to make sure you cut your ribbons long enough. Allow to dry.

12. Cut out the petals using the petal template. You will need 12 per flower.

13. Roll the petals back on themselves into

Fig. 3.

Fig. 4.

curls using a skewer or paint brush handle.
14. (Fig. 2.) Tacky glue the base of each petal and attach to the lower part of the bulb shape, under the last row of cone spikes, leaving no gap.

Making the calyx
15. Cut 2.5cm (1") wide ribbons from pale green crepe and outstretch. You will need 15-23cm (6"-9") lengths per flower. Follow the zigzag pattern on the calyx template.
16. Using a thick piece of stub wire, curl all the zigzag edges over in the same direction.
17. (Fig. 3 and 4.) Tacky glue the straight edge of the calyx and attach to the underside of the petals so they bend away from the flower with the zigzag tips facing

downwards. Wrap it 3 times round the flowers to form 3 rows of calyx.
18. Thicken the top 12cm (5") of the stem by wrapping floral tape around until it's approximately 1cm (½") thick. Graduate it to merge into the rest of the stem.

Making the leaves
19. Make leaves, using the template, if you want to add foliage.
20. Cut ribbons of green crepe to cover the stem from top to bottom.
21. Rub dark pink/purple pastel up and down the bottom ¾ of the stem and seal with a little matte sealant or glue.
22. Pull the petals downwards to create their distinctive droopy look.

echinacea double scoop 'lemon cream'

Echinacea 'Lemon Cream' is a hybrid, which means it has been produced by the cross-breeding of two different varieties. I chose this variety because of its soft lemon-yellow, double pom-pom flowers, which put on a sizzling show of colour in the garden and attract the attention of birds, bees and butterflies.

What you'll need

- Essential kit bag
- Glue gun
- Hot glue sticks
- Crepe paper in cream and soft yellows

See page 139 for templates

You guessed it! I love Echinacea.

This variety has soft lemon yellow pom-pom flowers with flared ray petals which create an attractive minimalist look in your home. Echinacea Double Scoop also comes in mandarin, raspberry, bubblegum and cranberry varieties.

Fig. 1.

Fig. 2.

HOW TO MAKE ECHINACEA DOUBLE SCOOP 'LEMON CREAM'

1. Tape 2 pieces of thick stub wire together to form a long stem and wrap it in a couple of layers of floral tape to thicken.

2. Bend the top over into a hook shape.

Making the florets

3. Cut out the central florets from pale yellow crepe, using the floret template.

4. Cut 5cm (2") lengths of thin stub wire.

5. Tacky glue each floret and wrap around the cut wire.

6. (Fig. 1.) Curl back each of the floret tips, using a piece of thick stub wire.

7. Glue the florets at the bases into 3's.

Making the cone

8. Cut a 3.5cm x 10cm (1½" x 4") piece of yellow crepe and fringe it.

9. (Fig. 2.) Tacky glue along the base, roll it up and hot glue to the top of the hook shape.

10. Cut a 2.5cm (1") length of dark green crepe.

11. (Fig. 3.) Using floral tape at the base of the fringed ribbon, wrap round and round the hook to form a bulb shape.

12. (Fig. 4.) Tacky glue the ribbon of green crepe and, starting from the base of the fringed roll, wrap the ribbon around, covering the glue and paper join.

13. (Fig. 5.) You can then start to add the

Fig. 3.

Fig. 4.

bunches of florets, sticking them into place with the green crepe ribbon. Add them evenly, leaving a small gap so they don't quite touch each other. Start in the centre and layer around it until it is covered from the top to the thickest part of the bulb.

Making the petals

14. Use a pale yellow crepe or colour cream crepe with a pale yellow medium and allow to dry.

15. Cut 7.5cm (3") ribbons from the crepe, outstretch and fold over 5 times. By putting 2 or 3 petal templates next to each other, you will be able to cut ten or more petals from each ribbon.

16. (Fig. 6.) Using the lines on the template as a guide, fold in the petals. Using a paper creaser gently run along the fold.

17. Careful unfold, ensuring you don't undo the creases.

18. Gently cup the petals near the base.

19. Using a skewer, curl all the petal tips backwards.

20. Glue the petal bases and stick them individually under the bottom row of florets.

21. Overlap some of them so that they all fit neatly around the whole central floret cone.

Making the calyx

22. Cut a 2.5cm (1") ribbon from pale green crepe.

23. Follow the pattern on the calyx template.

Fig. 5.

Fig. 6.

Fig. 7.

24. Once cut, fold all the spiky edges over a thick piece of stub wire making sure they are all are in the same direction.

25. (Fig. 7.) Tacky glue along the straight edge and wrap once around the base of the petals so the spikes fold downwards. Carefully wrap the next layer a little lower and the third below that to form 3 spiky layers for the Echinacea calyx.

Making the leaves

26. Make leaves, if you like the look of them, or just leave the stems bare.

Assembling the finished stem

27. Starting from the base of the calyx start to wrap floral tape around the stem. Once you have wrapped 5cm (2") down the stem, loop back and wrap again to thicken the top part of the stem.

28. (Fig. 8.) Pull the petals downwards and curl the edges and tips with a piece of thick stub wire.

29. Cut 2.5cm (1") ribbons of mid-green crepe and outstretch. Tacky glue along the length and, starting from the base of the calyx, wrap up and down the stem, covering the floral tape. If you are adding leaves, attach 2 opposite each other approximately halfway down the stem.

Double Scoop Echinaceas have eye-catching abundant flowers with double-layered petals in a clear lemon yellow on strong dark stem. They flower all through the summer into autumn

Fig. 8.

larkspur, 'annual delphinium'

Larkspur is such a tall, graceful flower and a classic British cottage garden staple. With its long stalks of blue blossoms, it is a great cut flower which adds variety and colour to any flower arrangement. It looks great mixed with other cottage flowers or in a display on its own.

What you'll need

- Essential kit bag
- Crepe paper in white, green and petal colour choice
- Green marker

See page 139 for templates

Tall spikes of coloured flowers and green feathery foliage make Larkspur one of my favourite flowers. They come in a variety of pretty colours.

This is one for anyone who love the classic jumble of flowers that typify the cottage garden look.

Fig. 1.

Fig. 2.

HOW TO MAKE LARKSPUR, 'ANNUAL DELPHINIUM'

Making the stem
1. Attach 2 pieces of thick stub wire together to make 1 long 140cm (55") stem with floral tape to form the stem.

Making the petals
2. (Fig. 1.) Choose or colour crepe paper for your Larkspur.

3. (Fig. 2.) Cut the smaller inner petals from a paler shade of the colour you have chosen.

4. Curl these little petals backwards around a thick piece of stub wire.

5. Cut the outer petals from the darker shade of the coloured crepe. Curl the petals around a thick piece of stub wire.

6. Cut a 1cm (½") ribbon of white crepe.

7. Colour a thin line along one edge, using a pale green marker.

8. Fine fringe along the green line.

9. Cut this ribbon into 2.5cm (1") pieces.

10. Cut 10-12 pieces of thin stub wire approximately 8cm (3") in length.

11. Glue along the straight edge of the fringed crepe and wrap it around the tip of the thin wire.

12. Apply glue to the bases of 6-8 of the inner petals and attach them evenly along the central fringing, overlapping the petals. Make around 12-14 flowers, keeping 3-4 to one side.

13. Take 10-14 outer petals, apply tacky

Fig. 3

Fig. 4.

glue to the bases and attach them evenly around the smaller inner petals. Repeat until they all have both inner and outer petals, with the exception of the 3-4 kept to one side.

Making the buds

14. To make buds for the top of the stem cut 3 x 7.5cm (3") pieces of thin stub wire.
15. Wrap the top 1cm (½") of the wire with floral tape and gently shape with your fingers into a bud like shape.
16. Cut 1cm (½") ribbons from green crepe.
17. Tacky glue along the ribbon and wrap it around the bud shape several times.
18. (Fig. 3.) Using some small sharp scissors snip an X-shape in the top of the

bud and fold the corners out to form an opening bud.

Making the spurs

19. Cut a 2.5cm (1") ribbon of coloured crepe and tacky glue along the whole length. Twist at each end to form a string length and allow to dry.
20. Cut the string into 2.5cm (1") lengths. You will need one length for each of the larger flowers.
21. Attach the string to the stem using tacky glue.
22. Cover the join with a spare outer petal.
23. (Fig. 4.) Gently curl the string up so to forms a upward flick.
24. Bend the wire down opposite the spur.

Fig. 5.

Fig. 6.

This wire forms the shape of the flower stem and is ready to attach to the main stem.

Making the stem

27. Wrap all the thin flower stems with a fine ribbon of green crepe.

28. Starting at the tip of the main stem, add a bud and secure with a tacky glued ribbon of green crepe. Be careful not to use too much tape as it will add too much bulk and the stem at the top will look too thick.

29. Just below the first bud add another.

30. (Fig. 5.) Working concentrically around the stem, first adding the buds, then the smaller pale flowers and finally the larger darker flowers at the bottom.

Assembling the finished stem

31. Once you have added all the flowers, finish wrapping the stem with crepe ribbon.

32. Cut about five 5cm x 12cm (2"x5") lengths of crepe and outstretch.

33. Fine fringe the lengths making the fringing a good 2.5cm (1") in length.

34. Place the fringing between your thumb and forefinger and rub gently together to ruffle it up. Do this along the whole length of the fringed strip.

35. Repeat for all the other lengths. These will form the lacy foliage.

36. Cut a pieces of thin wire into 5cm (2") lengths; one for each length of fringed crepe.

37. Tacky glue along the straight edge of the fringed lengths and wrap around the thin wire.

38. (Fig. 6.) Attach the foliage pieces with a ribbon of crepe in the same way as the flowers. Wrap the ribbon right to the end of the stem and cut off any excess.

alcalthaea suffrutescens, 'parkalee'

The Alcalthaea is a cross between a mallow and a hollyhock and is a thoroughly modern twist on the traditional cottage garden flower. It's a beautiful tall flower, with semi-double creamy apricot-pink flowers. The flowers have a pretty ruffle in the centre and purple tipped stamens.

What you'll need

- Essential kit bag
- Crepe paper in cream, green and pale pink
- Pastel in pale pink
- Maroon marker

See page 140 for templates

I love all flowers but this one stole my heart! The delicacy of the petals which form rosette-shaped blooms and their colouring are just beautiful. Like its relation the hollyhock, Alcalthaea can grow really big so don't be afraid to make a statement and make yours enormous!

Fig. 1.

Fig. 2.

HOW TO MAKE: ALCALTHAEA SUFFRUTESCENS 'PARKALEE'

1. Attach lengths of thick stub wire together using floral tape until you have the correct length of stem for your flowers.

2. Hook approximately 8 pieces of 10cm (4") medium thick stub wire.

3. (Fig. 1.) Using floral tape, wrap around the hook to make ball shapes. Repeat with all 8 pieces of wire.

Making the buds

4. Cut 4 bud covers from green crepe, using the bud cover template.

5. Cup and tacky glue the bud covers and attach them evenly over the ball of tape. The covers should all meet at the tip of the bud. Curl them using a piece of thick wire.

6. (Fig. 2.) For each bud, cut an outer calyx using the outer sepals template. Fold a ribbon of green crepe to create 8 layers. Cut around the template to create a concertina strip of sepals ready to wrap around the stem.

7. Apply tacky glue around the base of the calyx strip and attach it evenly around the base of the bud.

8. Bunch 5 of the buds together and using floral tape, attach them to the top of the main stem.

9. Attach the other 3 buds working your way around and down the top 7.5-10cm (3-4") of the main stem.

Fig. 3

Fig. 4.

Making the stamen

10. Hook 10cm (4") lengths of medium thick stub wire for each flower. You will want to make 8-10 flowers per stem.

11. Cut ribbons of cream crepe and colour along the top edge with maroon pen.

12. Fringe along the length.

13. (Fig. 3.) Tacky glue along the base of the fringed ribbon and wrap around the hook.

14. Repeat for all the flowers

Making the petals

15. Cut 10 petals from the No. 1 petal template from pale pink crepe.

16. Curl each petal inwards.

17. Apply tacky glue at the base of each petal and attach them evenly around the central fringing.

18. (Fig. 4.) Repeat this step, cutting 20 petals per flower from the No. 2 petal template from pale pink crepe and attaching them.

19. Cut 7 petals per flower from the No. 3 petal template from cream crepe.

20. Using a soft pale pink pastel, rub a little colour onto the inner petals.

22. Cup and curl each petal.

23. Apply a little tacky glue at the base and pinch the bases together.

24. Apply a little more glue and attach the petals evenly behind the No. 2 petals.

25. Cut 5 petals per flower using No. 4 petal template from cream crepe.

Fig. 5.

Fig. 6.

26. Rub a little of the soft pale pink pastel on the edges of some of the petals.

27. Cup and curl each petal.

28. Apply a little tacky glue and pinch at the base.

29. Attach each petal with a little tacky glue to the base at the back of the flower. I like to pop one at 12 o'clock, one at 2 o'clock and one at 7 o'clock. I then fill the gaps at 5 o'clock and 9 o'clock, with the remaining two petals slightly behind them.

Making the sepals

30. Cut 5 sepals per flower using the sepals inner template.

31. (Fig. 5.) Cup the sepals and attach them evenly to the back of the flower at the base of the petals.

32. Repeat the process to make and attach the outer sepals around the base of the inner sepals.

33. (Fig. 6.) Using floral tape attach the flowers individually, working your way around and down the stem until they are attached and distributed evenly.

Making the foliage

34. Follow the steps below if you would like to add foliage.

35. (Fig. 7.) Using the leaf template as a size guide, cut 3 squares from green crepe. Three squares will make 1 leaf.

36. Cut the squares in half along the diagonal.

Fig. 7

Fig. 8

37. Arrange the 3 squares to follow the direction of the grain on each template.
38. Glue 2 halves of the squares together with a piece of thin wire down the centre to create the leaf vein. Leave 2.5cm (1") extra length on the wire at the base of the join, once the 2 sections have been glued together. Medium thick stub wire should be used for the middle section; this will make the central leaf vein look bigger and also provide a bit more strength to the leaf.
39. Using the templates, cut LLeaf, RLeaf and MidLeaf from your 3 squares of green crepe paper.
40. Glue along both sides of the MidLeaf and attach LLeaf to the left and RLeaf to the right.

41. To hold in place, wrap a little tape around all 3 wires.
42. Cover over the floral tape and stalk with a ribbon of green crepe.
43. Allow to dry and repeat if you want to make more leaves.

Assembling the finished stem
44. (Fig. 6.) You can now shape your leaves and attach them to the main stem with a ribbon of tacky glue.

japanese anemone, 'honorine jobert'

I love this tall stately perennial which comes in a variety of shades from white to ivory and creamy pinks. Each flower has a distinctive green button at its centre. Anemones are late flowering so when everything else in the garden is wilting, these pretty flowers are still holding their heads high.

You will need

- Essential kit bag
- Crepe paper in white
- Glue gun
- Hot glue sticks
- Yellow chalk powder
- Orange chalk powder
- Green chalk powder
- Orange marker

See page 141 for templates

I have chosen this Japanese Anemone because I think it adds a little pure white simple elegance to the mix. The 'Honorine Jobert' has slightly larger flowers than the standard anemone so it always catches my eye. I love how, despite looking so delicate, they are actually strong, resilient flowers.

Fig. 1.

Fig. 2.

HOW TO MAKE: JAPANESE ANEMONE 'HONORINE JOBERT'

1. Take a length of thick stub wire and, using long nose pliers, curl into a loop at the top.
2. Use a glue gun, fill the loop with a ball of hot glue and allow to dry. Use the template labelled centre as a size guide.
3. Cut a thin strip of pale green crepe and apply tacky glue.
4. (Fig. 1.) Wrap neatly around the glue ball to cover it in green crepe.
5. Apply a thin layer of glue to the top and dust with a little pale green chalk powder.

Making the stamen

6. Cut a ribbon of white crepe, colour one edge with orange marker and fine fringe.
7. Dip the orange tips in a little glue and dust with yellow/orange chalk dust.
8. (Fig. 2.) Apply tacky glue along the unfringed edge.

Making the petals

9. Cut ribbons of white crepe and outstretch.
10. Fold over six times.
11. Cut out petals using the petal template.
12. Gently cup each petal.
13. (Fig. 3.) Using a skewer or something similar curl the petal edges
14. Tacky glue the bases and glue three petals around the centre, overlapping some and attaching a couple behind in the gaps.
15. Repeat this process with another three petals.

Fig. 3

Fig. 4.

16. Glue the bases and attach the 3 petals at the back of the flower.

17. Cover the stem with a ribbon of green crepe.

18. Bend the stem down 90 degrees at the back of the flower.

19. If you want more flowers on each stem, make more following the same steps.

Making the leaves

20. If you want to add leaves, cut a few from the different sized leaf templates. Add the smaller leaves approximately 12cm (5") down the stem. This is also where you should add extra flower heads if you are making multiple heads.

21. Fasten the leaves and flower stems together using floral tape.

Assembling the finished stem

22. Once you have made more stems, join them together 12cm (5") down the stem. Add a larger leaf at the join as I have done.

23. Secure using floral tape.

24. (Fig. 4.) Glue and wrap ribbons of green crepe evenly around the stems from top to bottom covering the floral tape.

climbing rose, 'perpetually yours'

Roses are a symbol of love and I love them! There are over 300 species of rose, so the choice is endless when it comes to deciding what rose you want to make. I chose 'Perpetually Yours' because it has a pretty country cottage look which means its very versatile. It would make a beautiful wedding rose.

You will need

- Essential kit bag
- Crepe paper in yellows, creams and green

See page 141 for templates

This is such a beautiful climbing rose. It sports fully double blooms in a range beautiful creams and pale yellows. Like all good cottage garden roses, it loves to climb. I have mine trailing around the front door of my house in Yorkshire.

Fig. 1.

Fig. 2.

HOW TO MAKE: CLIMBING ROSE 'PERPETUALLY YOURS'

1. Choose your crepe paper colours. I have used darker cream, vanilla and ivory shades.

2. Hook a piece of thick stub wire.

Making the stamen

3. Cut 2.5cm (1") ribbons from yellow/gold crepe. You will need 2 lengths per flower centre.

4. Fringe the ribbon.

5. Tacky glue the base of the fringed ribbon.

6. Wrap under and around the hook.

7. Use your thumb and finger to ruffle the fringing.

Making the petals

8. Using the darkest shade for the centre cut petals using the PER1 template. You will need approximately 12 stacks of 3 petals per flower centre.

9. Glue the base of each petal and stick them together in stacks of 3.

10. Apply a dot of tacky glue at the base of the stacks and pinch them together.

11. (Fig. 2.) Hot glue the base of a stack of petals and attach them evenly around the central fringing one at a time.

12. Bend the tops of 6 of the stacks over and attach with glue to the base, to create the look of unfurling centres.

13. Ruffle the other stacks gently.

Fig. 3

Fig. 4.

14. (Fig. 3.) Cut 12 petals from each of the PER2 templates (1, 2 and 3) and colour as you did for PER1 petals.

15. Cup each petal, and curl it inwards with thick slab wire.

16. Glue the base of one of each size petal.

17. Stack 1 of each of these petals in size order with the smallest on top. Add a dot of tacky glue at the base of the stack and pinch it together. You'll need 12 stacks per flower.

18. Hot glue the base of each stack and attach evenly around the centres. Attach some in the gaps behind others.

19. Repeat the steps to make petals from the PER3 templates.

20. Using your chosen paler coloured shades of crepe, cut 30 petals from the PER4 templates.

21. Keep 5 petals to one side.

22. Cup each petal.

23. Tacky glue and pinch the bases of each one. **(Fig. 4.)**

25. Curl the edges out.

26. Glue in 3's at the base. Stick 2 petals next to each other and then in the centre behind.

27. Take the 5 petals that were put to one side and reverse cup.

28. Glue the base and pinch inwards.

29. Curl the edges outwards, in the same way as the reverse cupping.

Fig. 5.

Fig. 6.

Making the sepals

30. Cut 5 sepals from green crepe, using the sepal template.

31. Cut little slits on the sepals, following the lines on the template.

32. Glue evenly around the base of the flower and attach the sepal bases to the stem. **(Fig. 5.)**

33. Curl each sepal backwards.

Making the ovary

34. Using floral tape wrap it 3 or 4 times around the base of the flower to make a small ball shape.

Assembling the finished stem

35. If you are adding leaves make them using the leaf template.

36. Cut ribbons of green crepe and tacky glue them. **(Fig. 6.)**

37. Wrap the green crepe ribbon from the calyx to the bottom of the stem, adding any leaves as you go.

clematis, 'integrifolia alba'

Known as the "Queen of the Climbers", the Clematis is a member of the buttercup family. There are a huge number of varieties of Clematis and they come in every colour and size you can imagine. I chose an 'Integrifolia Alba' for its pretty, white, bell-shaped blooms.

You will need

■ Essential kit bag

■ Crepe paper in white and green

See page 142 for templates

The Clematis 'Integrifolia Alba' is a low growing clematis that will happily scramble in a border over other planting. It has dainty nodding bell-shaped white flowers with an occasional tinge of blue at the base and a lovely scent. I love using climbers to add trailing shapes to my bouquets and flower arrangements.

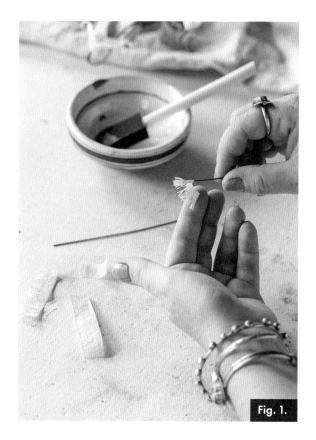

Fig. 1.

Fig. 2.

HOW TO MAKE: CLEMATIS 'INTEGRIFOLIA ALBA'

Making the stamens

1. Cut 1cmx5cm (½"x2") ribbons from white crepe.

2. Colour along the bottom half using pale green.

3. Fringe the ribbon.

4. Glue along the base of the fringed ribbon.

5. (Fig. 1.) Take a piece of thin wire at least 15cm (6") in length and wrap the fringed ribbon around the top to form the central stamen.

6. Cut 2.5cmx5cm (1"x 2") ribbons from yellow crepe.

7. Tacky glue the base.

8. Wrap around the green/white centre.

Making the petals

9. Cut 7.5x10cm (3"x4") ribbons from white crepe. Be careful not to outstretch.

10. Fold in half and then half again. This will give you 4 petals.

11. (Fig. 2.) Use the petal template to cut the petals (4 per flower). Fold along the lines shown on the template.

12. Cup each petal at the widest part.

13. Using a piece of thick stub wire, curl the tips of each petal. Curl some outward and some inwards.

14. Glue each petal at the base.

15. (Fig. 3.) Attach 2 petals opposite each other and then attach the final 2 in between them, opposite each other.

Fig. 3

Fig. 4.

16. Cut narrow ribbons from green crepe and wrap round the base of the petals to cover where they have been attached. Now wrap round to cover the whole stem.

17. Repeat until you have the required number of flowers on your stem.

Making the leaves

18. Make some leaves using the leaf templates.

Assembling the finished stem

19. Using a medium thick piece of stub wire for the main stem, begin attaching the flowers with floral tape.

20. At each joint where you attach flowers to the stem, add 2 leaves. You should use smaller leaves at the top of the stem.

21. To create longer climbing or trailing lengths, keep adding lengths of medium thick stub wire to the ends of the main stem and fasten with floral tape.

22. (Fig. 4.) To finish, cover the main stem by wrapping ribbons of glued green crepe over the top of the floral tape.

verbascum, 'southern charm'

The common name for Verbascum is Mullien. It is a hairy biennial plant that can grow up to two metres tall. It produces insect-friendly long flowering spikes in delicate eye-catching shades of peach, pink, lilac and apricot, with darker eyes and is very much on trend at the moment.

What you'll need

- Essential kit bag
- Crepe paper in purple, cream
- Paints, pastels or inks to colour your own papers in peach, lavender, café au lait,
- Brown chalk powder

See page 142 for templates

'Southern Charm' is a beautiful and unusual variety of Verbascum and one of my favourite plants. It just adds something a little different to paper flower making.

The graceful flower spikes smothered with uniquely coloured flowers with fluffy purple centres are beautiful. Feel fee to pack your stems as sparsely or densely as you like.

Fig. 1.

Fig. 2.

HOW TO MAKE: VERBASCUM, 'SOUTHERN CHARM'

Making the stem

1. Cut a ribbon of mid to dark green crepe.

2. Glue the ribbon and wrap it around a medium thick length of stub wire.

3. Cut upside down V-shapes into the top 5cm (2") of the wire by snipping downwards with small sharp scissors.

Making the buds

4. For the little buds at the top of the stem take a 7.5cm (3") length of thin green wire.

5. (Fig. 1.) Glue and wrap a fine strip of cream or purple crepe ribbon to the tip of the wire, forming it into small balls to make bulb shapes. Make as many as you like, using the bud templates for size guides.

Making the petals

6. Colour your crepe. Verbasum comes in the most beautiful colours, so have fun with your mediums and mix them up.

7. Decide how many flowers you want on your stem.

8. Cut your petals using the petal templates. You will need 5 petals per flower.

9. Fold each petal in half and form a central crease from base to tip. This crease is the front of the petal. They are small petals so you may need to use fine tweezers to hold them as you crease them.

10. With a piece of thick stub wire carefully curl the edges of the tiny petals. Curl some inwards and others outward, trying to keep

Fig. 3

Fig. 4.

the creases in the centre of your petals. Put your petals aside to use later.

Making the centres

11. For the centres, you will need to cut 4 of the tiny inner template shapes per flower from purple crepe.

12. Very carefully fringe around each of the edges, using tweezers to hold them steady.

13. Put the purple centres aside to use later.

Making the flowers

14. (Fig. 2.) Cut 7.5cm (3") lengths of thin green wire and dip the tips into glue and then some brown chalk dust.

15. Apply tacky glue to the base of 4 of the purple centre petals.

16. (Fig. 3.) Attach the purple centre petals about 1cm (½") below the brown chalky tip.

17. Use tweezers to attach the petals onto the stem wire.

18. (Fig. 4.) Glue the bases of 5 of the petals that you set aside earlier and attach them evenly next to each other around the purple centres. You may need tweezers to secure them to the stalk.

Fig. 5.

Fig. 6.

Making the calyx
19. (Fig. 5.) Cut the tiny calyx from green crepe paper, using the bud calyx template for the buds and flower calyx template for the flowers.
20. (Fig. 6.) Glue the calyx at the base and apply them to the back of the flower using tweezers.

Assembling the finished stem
21. (Fig. 7.) Cut ribbons of green crepe and glue them, starting at the top of the stem under the precut V shapes. Add a bud at the top, securing with the ribbon. Wrap the ribbon round and down the stem, before adding another bud. Work your way down the stem adding buds and then flowers until the stem is covered. Leave a length of stem without flowers, depending on how tall you want your stems to be.

Verbascum can grow
to about two metres
in the garden so make
sure you create a long
stem to make your
flower look authentic

Fig. 7.

wallflower, 'sunset purple'

The 'Sunset Purple' Wallflower is a beautiful spring flower with a delicious scent and unusual purple blooms which change colour as they age. Sadly, they are short lived so making them in paper is the perfect way of keeping them alive for longer!

What you'll need

■ Essential kit bag

■ Crepe paper in green, purple, apricot

■ Paints, pastels or inks in purples, peach and apricot

See page 142 for templates

Can you believe these little beauties belong to the cabbage family? They immediately transport me back to my childhood. Growing up in Runswick Bay on the Yorkshire Coast, these sweet smelling sea-air loving flowers grew from every crack in all the walls and paving slabs.

Wallflowers come in a wealth of colours so it is a flower you can really enjoy experimenting with. I have made them in all sorts of colours, including purple and apricot.

Fig. 1.

Fig. 2.

HOW TO MAKE: WALLFLOWER, 'SUNSET PURPLE'

1. Cut 5 7.5cm (3") lengths of thin wire.

Making the buds

2. Cut some thin ribbons from green crepe.

3. Apply tacky glue on the ribbon and wrap it around the top of the wire to make 5 small ball shapes for the buds at the top of the stems.

4. (Fig. 1.) Bunch all 5 buds together and secure them to the top of a length of medium thick stub wire with floral tape, using the bud template as a guide.

5. Choose a purple crepe or colour your choice of crepe with a purple shade. I used a mix of purple and apricot crepe coloured with purple paint.

6. Cut around 20 x 5cm (2") lengths of thin green wire.

7. Cut 3 to 5 1cm x 5cm (½" x 2") lengths of coloured ribbon.

8. Tacky glue and wrap a length of ribbon around one of your thin pieces of wire.

9. Using small sharp scissors cut into the tops of the wrapped paper, splaying and curling them to form unfurling buds.

Making the petals

10. Cut lots of petals using the petal template.

11. Crumple the petals. Uncrumple them and then curl the edges in different directions, cupping some of them.

120

Fig. 3

Fig. 4.

12. (Fig. 2.) Stick 4 petals evenly around each length of cut wire.

Making the calyx
13. To make the calyx cut 2.5cm x 1cm (1" x ½") wide pieces from outstretched green crepe.
14. In the direction of the grain fold the crepe in half and then half again.
15. Cut a V-shape from the centre point of the top edge to half way down the paper.
16. When you unfold the paper, you will be left with a skinny zigzag piece.
17. (Fig. 3.) Tacky glue along the straight edge and wrap the paper around the back of the flower at the base of the petals.
18. Make the calyx for all of the flowers.

Making the leaves
19. Follow the leaf templates if you want to add leaves.

Assembling the finished stem
20. (Fig. 4.) Cut ribbons from green crepe and outstretch it.
21. Tacky glue the ribbon and, starting just below the 5 buds at the tip, wrap around the stem. Add unfurling buds along the stem, followed by the flowers
22. Add any leaves by tucking them in to the ribbon once you have added all the flowers. Bend the stem a little to give it shape and manipulate until you are happy with the position and shape of the flowers.

china rose, 'rosa mutabilis'

This stunning rose is a classic China rose which flowers on and off for six months of the year. Its name comes from the Latin word for changing, 'mutantur' because the petals change colour - opening as a pretty pink and fading to a delicate apricot colour.

What you'll need

- Essential kit bag
- Crepe paper in yellow, orange, pale yellow, cream, pinks, green
- Paints and inks in pinks
- Pastels in yellow, peach, dark pink

See page 143 for templates

The China rose is one of my favourite roses. I just adore how delicate it is. It's a climber, so it is also a great plant for adding shape to your displays.

It's such a unique rose, producing single scented flowers that change colour as they age. The flowers look just like butterflies perching on branches.

123

Fig. 1.

Fig. 2.

HOW TO MAKE: CHINA ROSE, 'ROSA MUTABILIS'

1. Hook a medium thick piece of stub wire

Making the pistil and stamens
2. Cut 2.5cm (1") lengths of ribbon from orange/yellow crepe (younger flowers) and pale yellow crepe (older flowers).
3. Colour the top of the longest side of the pale yellow ribbon with a line of brown pen. Finely fringe the ribbon, cutting through the pen line to create the anther.
4. Tacky glue along the base of the fringing.
5. (Fig. 1.) Wrap the fringed ribbon over the wire hook to cover it.

Making the petals
6. Colour your crepe. I dipped 7.5cm (3") of some of my lengths of cream crepe ribbon in pale pink water based paint and ink and others in darker shades of pink.
7. Cut the petals from these coloured ribbons using the petal template. You will need 5 petals per flower.
8. Cup your petals.
9. Rub some creamy yellow and peach pastels into your cups.
10. Using thick stub wire, curl the petals over backwards either side of the V-shape at the centre of the top of each petal template.
11. (Fig. 2.) Apply a little tacky glue at the

124

Fig. 3

Fig. 4.

base of each petal and pinch them together. **12.** Apply a little more glue at the base and attach a petal at 12 o'clock. Attach another at 5 o'clock. Then attach a petal behind these two petals. Add another at 10 o'clock, slightly behind the 12 o'clock petal and then attach the final petal between the 5 o'clock and 10 o'clock petals.

Making the sepals
13. Cut the sepals from green crepe paper, using the sepal template. I used a green doublette, with the darker shade on the outside. You will need 5 per flower.
14. Rub a little dark pink pastel into the inner side of the sepals.
15. Cup each sepal gently.

16. (Fig. 3.) Apply a little tacky glue to the bases of the sepals and attach them evenly to the back of the bases of the petals.

Assembling the finished stem
17. (Fig. 4.) Wind a little floral tape at the base of the flower, just under the sepals, to thicken that section of the stem.
18. Cut ribbons of green crepe and tacky glue them.
19. Wrap the whole stem in green crepe.
20. Add leaves if desired, using the leaf template for shape and pattern. You can add more flower heads to the stem to add shape and length if you want bigger stems or just stick to single stems, which look wonderful displayed in vases.

hellebore, 'christmas rose'

Did you know Hellebores belong to the buttercup family? They are absolutely beautiful and come in green, pink, gold and burgundy shades - some even have freckles. They are easy to grow but can be temperamental as cut flowers so they are wonderful flower to transform into paper.

What you'll need

- Essential kit bag
- Crepe paper in cream, white, greens
- Air dry clay
- Acrylic paint in greens
- Glue gun
- Hot glue sticks
- Pastel in pale green

See page 143 for templates

Commonly called 'Winter Rose', 'Christmas Rose' or 'Lenten Rose', these sweet little flowers burst into life during the winter months, adding a much needed pop of colour to cold grey days.

What look like petals are actually the sepals of this plant. These sepals protect the flower. To make it easy to follow, I have referred to them as petals in these instructions.

Fig. 1.

Fig. 2.

HOW TO MAKE: HELLEBORE, 'CHRISTMAS ROSE'

Making the seed pods

1. (Fig. 1.) Form small lumps of air dry clay into 3 seed pod shapes for the centre of the flower, using the seed pod template as a guide for shape. Seed pods can vary in size, so make a variety of sizes.

2. Push a thin piece of wire through the centre of each seed pod until it protrudes from the narrow top. Leave a 7.5cm (3") length of wire at the bottom for attaching.

3. Allow the clay to dry and paint green.

4. Bunch the seed pods, with the curve on the outer edge and the wire curling outwards.

5. Take a piece of thick stub wire for the main stem and hot glue the seed pod wires to it at the bottom. Allow to dry.

Making the sepals

6. (Fig. 2.) Wrap the join you have just created by gluing the thick wire to the thin wire of the seed pods using floral tape, this will provide a little more strength.

7. Cut a 4 x 7.5cm (1½" x 3") ribbon from cream or white crepe.

8. Run a thin pale green line along the top edge of the long edge.

9. Fine fringe, cutting through the green line.

10. Apply tacky glue along the base of the fringed ribbon and wrap it around the main stem, at the base of the seed pods, to form the sepals.

Fig. 3

Fig. 4.

Making the honey petals

11. Cut the honey petals from pale green crepe using the honey petal template. You will need 8-12 petals per flower.

12. (Fig. 3.) Starting at the base of the petal, fold one side over the other and glue. Apply a little more glue and, using gentle pressure, attach the honey petals under the sepals. Repeat until you have surrounded the sepals with honey petals.

Making the petals

13. Cut a ribbon of cream/white crepe the right size for the petal template.

14. Cut 5 petals, using the petal template.

15. Rub a little pale green pastel around the base and up into the centre on both sides of the petal.

16. Cup each petal and curl the edges inwards with a piece of thick stub wire.

17. Tacky glue the bases.

18. (Fig. 4.) Place 1 petal at 10 o'clock, 1 at 2 o'clock and 1 at 7 o'clock.

19. Place a petal behind, between 2 and 7 o'clock.

20. Finally, add a petal between 10 and 2 o'clock.

Assembling the finished stem

21. Cover over the petal bases and wrap the stem with a ribbon of tacky glued green crepe.

using your paper flowers

There are so many wonderful ways you can display your finished flowers. They create stunning interior decorations, make wonderful gifts and are perfect for special celebrations like weddings.

WRAPPING PRESENTS
Paper flowers are such a great way to decorate your presents. Do away with plastic ribbons and wrap your presents with recycled paper and a paper flower for decoration! Your flowers make a bonus gift.

A BOUQUET (OPPOSITE) Being a florist is my day job so I have to show you a gorgeous bouquet of flowers. Why wouldn't you want your wedding bouquet to be made from paper blooms so you can keep it forever? I often get asked to recreate wedding bouquets as a paper anniversary gift. It is such a lovely idea.

A VASE OF FLOWERS

A floral display makes everyone smile. A vase of flowers means you can have a forever display in your home and also show off your new found craft!

IKEBANA
Ikebana is a traditional Japanese method of flower arranging or 'giving life to flowers' that I have admired for years. A subtle, sensitive approach to flower arranging, the Japanese use differing heights of branches, blossoms and stems to create beautiful works of art.

1. poppy (page 32)

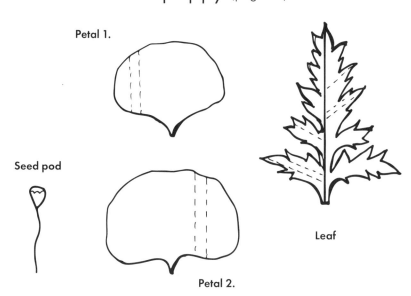

Petal 1.

Seed pod

Leaf

Petal 2.

2. evening primrose (page 36)

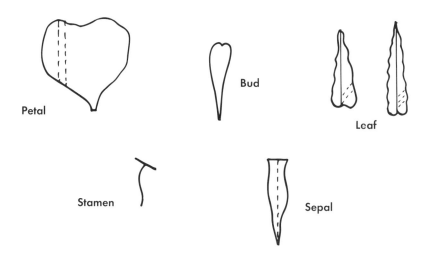

Petal

Bud

Leaf

Stamen

Sepal

3. floribunda rose (page 42)

Petals

1.

2.

Sepal

Leaf

2.

2.

3.

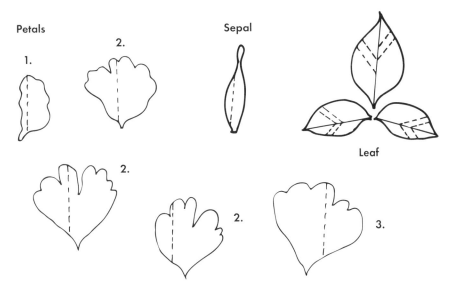

4. geum (page 48)

Petals

1.

2.

Sepal

Leaf sizes

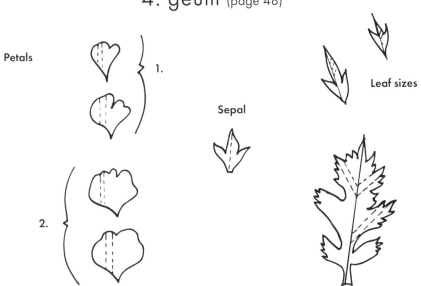

5. dahlia (page 52)

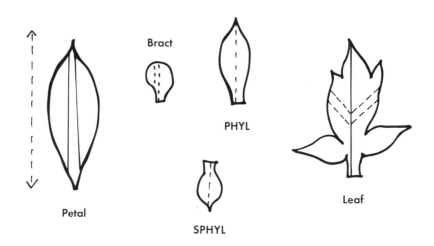

Bract

PHYL

Petal

SPHYL

Leaf

6. rowan berries (page 58)

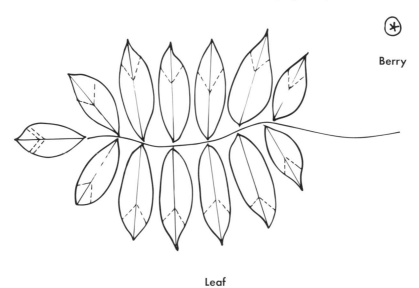

Berry

Leaf

7. musk rose (page 62)

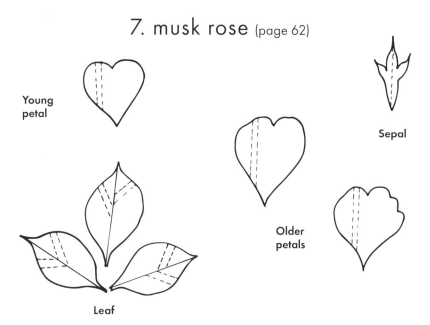

Young petal

Sepal

Older petals

Leaf

8. cherry blossom (page 66)

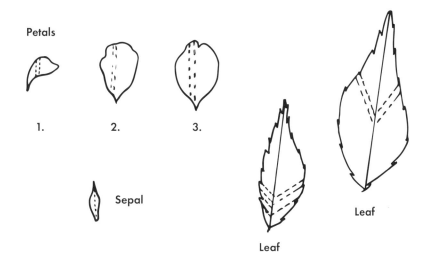

Petals

1.

2.

3.

Sepal

Leaf

Leaf

9. hydrangea (page 72)

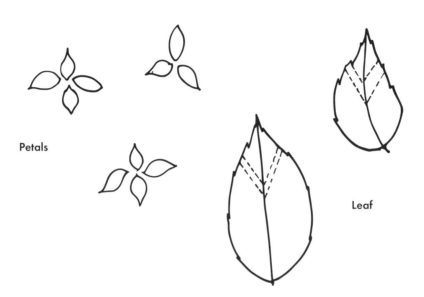

Petals

Leaf

10. echinacea pallida (page 76)

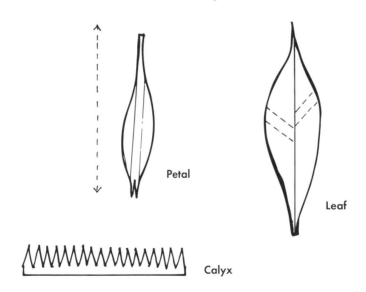

Petal

Leaf

Calyx

11. echinacea double scoop (page 80)

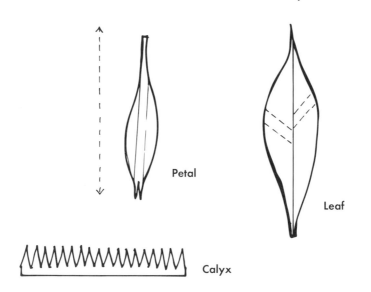

Petal

Leaf

Calyx

12. larkspur (page 86)

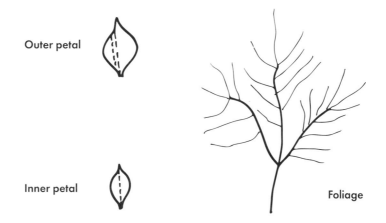

Outer petal

Inner petal

Foliage

13. alcalthaea suffrutescens (page 92)

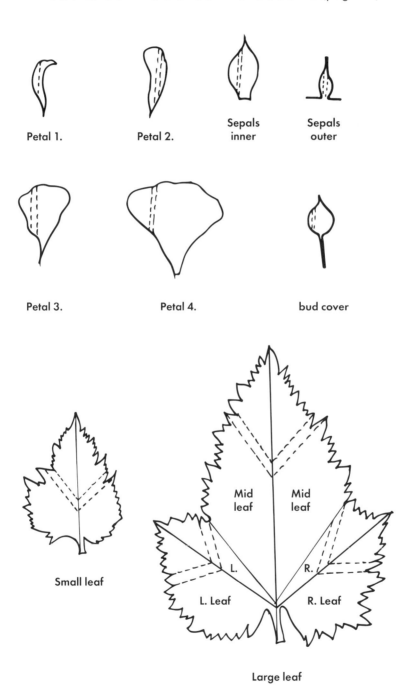

Petal 1.

Petal 2.

Sepals inner

Sepals outer

Petal 3.

Petal 4.

bud cover

Small leaf

Mid leaf

Mid leaf

L.

R.

L. Leaf

R. Leaf

Large leaf

14. japanese anemone (page 98)

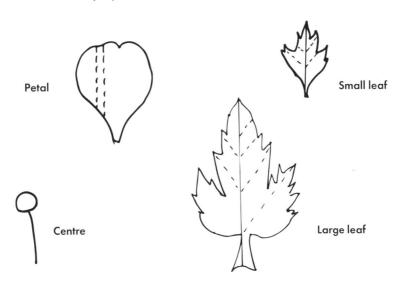

Petal

Small leaf

Centre

Large leaf

15. climbing rose (page 102)

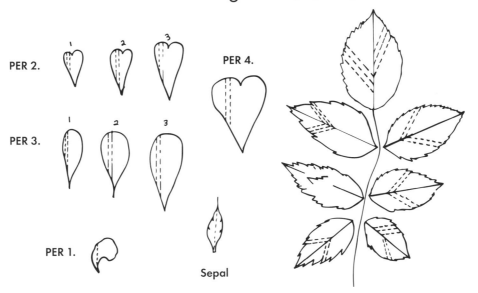

PER 2.

PER 4.

PER 3.

PER 1.

Sepal

16. clematis (page 108)

Petal

Top leaf

Lower leaf

17. verbascum (page 112)

Top buds

Lower buds

Bud calyx

Flower calyx

Petal

Inner

18. wallflower (page 118)

Buds

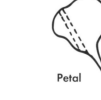

Petal

Leaf

19. china rose (page 122)

Petal

Leaf

Sepal

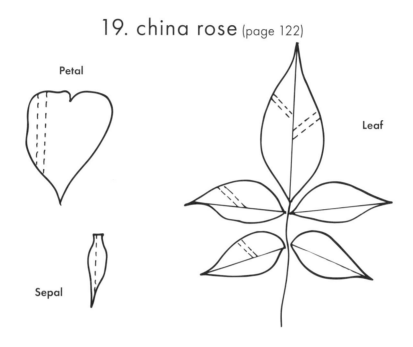

20. hellebore (page 126)

Seed Pod

Petal

Honey

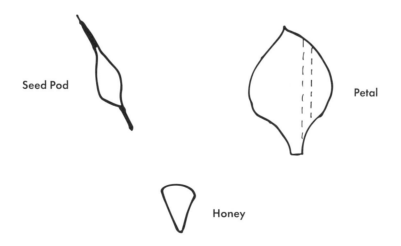

About the author

Sophie was born and raised by the sea in Runswick Bay, close to Whitby on the North Yorkshire coast. Born into a successful entrepreneurial family, it wasn't long before she was to follow her own calling and establish a floristry business, 'Ginger & Flynn', named after one of her sons and her ginger hair!

Sophie lives with her husband, Andy, and four boys, Hughie, Flynn, Samson and Kit. They have four dogs, chickens, a cat and a horse, 'Lady' - and their lifestyle is just the right balance of mayhem and love.

Sophie's home is her workplace, and being tucked away in the North Yorkshire Moors, surrounded by nature deeply inspires her work and everyday creativity.

Acknowledgements Thank you to Andy and my boys for putting up with my long days and nights working. To my amazing brother, Sandy, and my best friend, Tink, who were only a press of a button away for moral support and a constant source of creative inspiration. Thank you to my lovely friend Ceri for proofreading and for walks and sea swims to calm my nerves. To Zach and Grace (www.zachandgrace.co.uk) for working with me over the years and for their amazing eye for photography. To Geri (www.smugglerstreasures.co.uk) for my gorgeous jewellery. To Rachel (rachelinthedales.co.uk), who I commissioned to make the beautiful bowl for the Japanese anemone. To Emma (www.emmastothard.com) for the beautiful artwork in some of the pictures. To Louise (www. louisecondondesigns.co.uk) for her fabulous vases and positive support of my work. To the lovely Les, who I met through my business and whose work I loved the minute I saw it - many of the pots featured in the book were made by Les. To Annabel and Phillip, for providing me with the confidence to write this book, for friendship, support and for the constant encouragement and who I have had the pleasure of working with on projects for Love my Dress (www.lovemydress.net). Phillip grows all the flowers @moodwindflowers that provide me with a constant source of inspiration. We share the same ethics and passion for flowers and work together on weddings and events using his organically grown beautiful British flowers. To Jess, Sally, Anna, Laura and Julie for listening to me moan and for having the kids and horse to give me time to create and write. To Katherine, Jane and Aileen for all their help putting the book together.